A CHART

of the

COASTS, BAYS and HARBOURS

in

NEWFOUNDLAND

P.ᵗ FEROLLE.

...gh Pallisser Esq.ʳ

...James Cook.

Part of the Main

Part of the Main

An Illustrated History of
Newfoundland and Labrador

PETER NEARY
PATRICK O'FLAHERTY

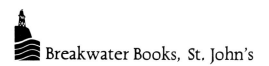
Breakwater Books, St. John's

The title of this book is derived from John Donne's Meditation XVII, 1624.

ENDLEAF: COURTESY HYDROGRAPHIC DEPARTMENT, MINISTRY OF DEFENCE, TAUNTON, SOMERSET.

CANADIAN CATALOGUING IN PUBLICATION DATA

Neary, Peter, 1938-
    Part of the main

Bibliography: p.
ISBN 0-919519-27-X

1. Newfoundland – History.   2. Labrador (Nfld.) –
History.   3. Newfoundland – Anniversaries, etc.
I. O'Flaherty, Patrick, 1939-   II. Title.

FC 2161.N42   971.8   C83-098498-4
F1123.N42

FRONT COVER PHOTO: Donald Lane
DESIGN: Brant Cowie/Artplus Ltd.

Printed and bound in Canada by
Herzig Somerville Ltd.

CONTENTS

PREFACE

NATIONAL MUSEUM OF NATURAL SCIENCES

Black Swallowtail and Alexis Butterflies

g? Newfoundland.

A drawing from Philip Henry
Gosse's "Entomologia Terrae
Novae" (1828-35).

IN RECENT YEARS, Newfoundland history has been approached from many points of view. This book, we hope, will add a fresh dimension to the work already done in the field. Our purpose was not only to illustrate the history of Newfoundland and Labrador as it is known, but to open up new sources for the province's visual history. We have been surprised by the volume of material we have found and hope that our initiative will lead to further archival and scholarly inquiry. Our book begins and ends with discovery, and our making of it has been an adventure.

Our first acknowledgement is to our immediate and extended families, who have stayed with us through another turn of the buoys. We thank Dr. Leslie Harris, the president of the Memorial University of Newfoundland, who saw in a moment the potential value of what we intended and supported us generously. The Department of History at the University of Western Ontario and the Department of English Language and Literature at Memorial University have been our principal bases of operation, and we are most grateful to Professor A.M.J. Hyatt and Professor D.G. Pitt. For typing assistance with the manuscript, we thank Betty Miller, Cathy Murphy, and Cathy Dooley of the English Department, Memorial University. A detailed list of the many other people and institutions contributing to this book is given in the credits. We single out here those who gave sustained and specialized help: Professor Gordon Handcock, C.F. Rowe, and Edward Rowe; ETV Photography, Memorial University, especially Jack Martin; the Newfoundland Museum, especially Jane Sproull-Thomson; the A.C. Hunter Library, in particular Mona Cram; the Centre for Newfoundland Studies, Queen Elizabeth II Library, Memorial University, where Anne Hart, Nancy Grenville, and Marian Burnett were most generous; Parks Canada, especially Ellen Earles; the Newfoundland Archives; and the Public Archives of Canada, especially Peter Robertson.

PETER NEARY / PATRICK O'FLAHERTY 1982

NEWFOUNDLAND AND LABRADOR are "a rough thing from God's hand." The island, 112,299 square kilometres in area and with a coastline cut into innumerable bays and inlets, presents a spectacular and menacing appearance from the North Atlantic. The novelist R.T.S. Lowell captured its character well; after visiting Conception Bay in the 1840s, he wrote, "The huge island stands, with its sheer, beetling cliffs, out of the ocean, a monstrous mass of rock and gravel, almost without soil, like a strange thing from the bottom of the great deep, lifted up, suddenly, into sunshine and storm, but belonging to the watery darkness out of which it has been reared."

Newfoundland may not seem companionable, but it can surprise and delight with its sudden bounteousness. The poet E.J. Pratt recalled just this aspect. Twenty years after leaving Newfoundland, he was still homesick for "the smell of kelp and fresh caplin in the coves; wind-swept barrens with square leagues of partridge berries; marshes at twilight with whirring snipe; herds of caribou crossing streams; miles of flakes with drying cod; and above all the Atlantic rolling its silver cascades over the beaches." Echoing Pratt's sentiments, the novelist Margaret Duley wrote, "How magnificent the country can look, how big and bold, and how strong of light." And so Newfoundland is.

Labrador, the island's continental counterpart and the province's northern frontier (a territory of 292,218 square kilometres) is said to have the most severe climate, within its latitudes, of any part of the world. It has never been for the timid, but it has long stirred the imaginative. Its coasts, extending northward to the fierce Torngat range of mountains and Cape Chidley, are North America's Atlantic battlements. The interior is a warped plateau, the very definition of the Canadian Shield. Until the nineteenth century, this region was the sole preserve of the Naskapi-Montagnais; no European ventured across the wild peninsula until 1834. Yet, for all its harshness, Labrador also abounds in its rivers, forests, ocean, and in the rock beneath its stern exterior. "However bleak the Labrador," the Canadian writer Norman Duncan wrote in 1904, "however naked and desolate that shore, flowers bloom upon it." And so it is.

The essence of Newfoundland's and Labrador's history is to be found in a series of accommodations to this remorseless and forbidding, but at moments unexpectedly felicitous, environment. Man has indeed left his mark on the region, but it is a small mark. Flying over the province today, one is struck by the still primitive landscape. There are no townships, quarter sections, or old seigniorial boundaries here; only frail, disordered trickles of settlement, with an occasional larger cluster of life. As Margaret Duley pointed out, Newfoundland is the creature, and "the people on her crust merely appendages." Oil rigs arrive, helicopters come and go, rivers are pent up, but the sea is untamed and the terrain remains primeval. The elements press in, the quarrel with them "an unnegotiated thing." It is an atmosphere which induces at once bravado and humility, mostly the latter.

Over the centuries, Newfoundlanders and Labradorians have crept into the farthest reaches of their homeland, but they are still mainly a northern people of the foreshore. Whatever technology has brought, doors are still "held ajar in storms." From the ancient first inhabitants to the present-day adventurers on the offshore, there is a continuity of experience. That is what this book is about.

Part of the Main

Tending fish, one of the many
tasks performed by women in
the outport economy of
Newfoundland.

CHAPTER ONE

PREHISTORY AND EUROPEAN DISCOVERY

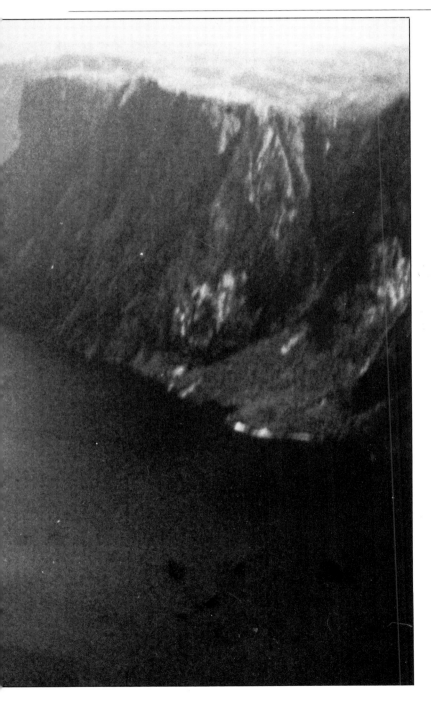

The Maritime Archaic People

THE LAST GREAT ICE AGE reached its peak in Labrador about 10,000 B.C. Slowly, over the following six millennia, the ice cap withdrew, and by 4,000 B.C. it had disappeared. As the ice moved back from the Labrador shore, the coastline was revealed in its now familiar terrain: rounded hills, ragged inlets of the sea, numerous small islands, bedrock scraped and denuded of topsoil, and the litter of glacial debris. It was hardly a hospitable environment; yet even as the ice cap was retreating from the coast, man appeared. Archaeological evidence shows that human life existed in southern Labrador around 7000 B.C. These first settlers appear to have been caribou-hunting Indians who moved northward from the Maritime provinces, crossed the mouth of the St. Lawrence River, and migrated along the north shore of the gulf. As they entered coastal Labrador, they could undoubtedly see the huge ice sheet that still existed inland and feel its chilling effect upon the climate. In time, their mode of life changed to adapt to these harsh new conditions.

By 5500 B.C. these Indian migrants to Labrador had evolved a lifestyle which is identifiable within the context of early North American peoples. Belonging to what is termed the Maritime Archaic Tradition, they lived by hunting, fishing, and gathering. Eventually, these people spread northward along the Labrador coast to Saglek Bay, and southward to the island of Newfoundland, where the earliest known traces of human life date from around 3000 B.C. Maritime Archaic burial sites at Port au Choix on the island's Great Northern Peninsula and L'Anse Amour in southern Labrador have provided archaeologists with a great number of artifacts from which to picture the Indians' habits as hunters and their relationship to their surroundings. Some of the objects discovered reveal a considerable sophistication in domestic and artistic ability. The site at Port au Choix, for example, contained an elaborate set of bone sewing implements, an antler comb in the shape of a merganser duck, and a representation of a killer whale, sculpted from igneous rock. The whale effigy is an object of great beauty. As hunters, the Maritime Archaic people had developed, among other weapons, an ingenious toggling harpoon which enabled them to hold seals and other prey after the initial wounding.

What eventually happened to the Maritime Archaic people remains a mystery; but they were probably the ancestors of the Beothuck Indians of the island of Newfoundland, and possibly also of the Naskapi-Montagnais of Labrador.

A 4000-year-old killer whale artifact, identified by its prominent dorsal fin, from an excavation at Port au Choix, Newfoundland. The 1968 dig in which it was discovered – part of a recent rebirth of interest in the archaeology of Newfoundland and Labrador – was supervised by Dr. James Tuck, author of *Newfoundland and Labrador Prehistory* (National Museum of Man, 1976). He has speculated that the killer whale was a cult object among the Maritime Archaic people.

ETV/MUN

The Dorset Eskimos

ONE REASON FOR THE DECLINE of the Maritime Archaic culture in Labrador may have been the appearance on the northern coast, around 2000 B.C., of a completely different race – the Palaeo-Eskimos. They were descendents of emigrants from Alaska who had spread throughout the Canadian Arctic following their arrival from Asia in the distant past. The first wave of these Eskimo people moved southward over hundreds of years, possibly as far as Hamilton Inlet, and then faded. Another group of the same people followed; these were the Dorset Eskimos, a culture that was widely dispersed around the coast of Newfoundland from approximately 500 B.C. to A.D. 600 (when it disappears from the island's archaeological record) and in coastal Labrador from approximately 500 B.C. to A.D. 1500. Around 1500, soon after the coming of the Inuit, the Dorset Eskimo culture in Labrador also mysteriously vanished.

Excavation of Dorset sites has revealed numerous artifacts, including exquisite miniature carvings of the animals hunted, carefully crafted small tools, and occasional human figurines. Amulets and masks apparently served some religious function. The Dorset Eskimos' delicate artwork is intriguing and memorable.

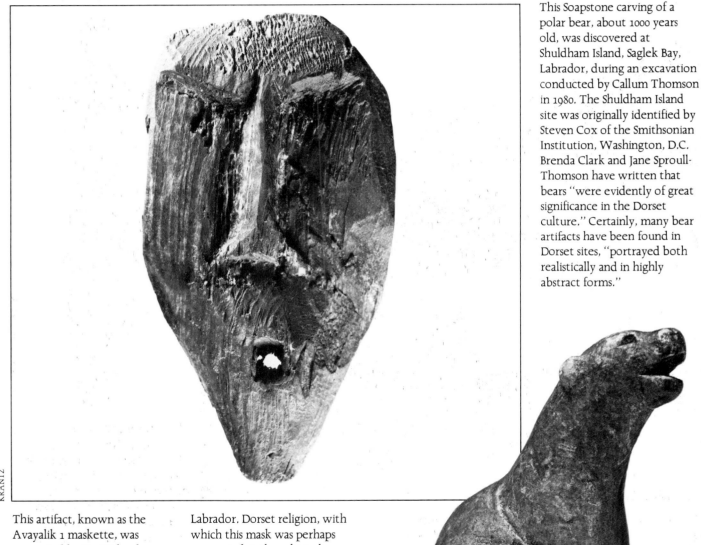

SMITHSONIAN INSTITUTION/VICTOR KRANTZ

NFLD. MUSEUM/ANTONIA McGRATH

This artifact, known as the Avayalik 1 maskette, was excavated by Dr. Richard Jordan of Bryn Mawr College, Pennsylvania, while leading a field party of the Smithsonian-Bryn Mawr Torngat Archaeological Project in 1978. It was found on the Avayalik Islands, north of Saglek Bay, Labrador. Dorset religion, with which this mask was perhaps connected, is thought to have been animistic, human and animal life being governed by spirits.

This Soapstone carving of a polar bear, about 1000 years old, was discovered at Shuldham Island, Saglek Bay, Labrador, during an excavation conducted by Callum Thomson in 1980. The Shuldham Island site was originally identified by Steven Cox of the Smithsonian Institution, Washington, D.C. Brenda Clark and Jane Sproull-Thomson have written that bears "were evidently of great significance in the Dorset culture." Certainly, many bear artifacts have been found in Dorset sites, "portrayed both realistically and in highly abstract forms."

The Inuit

THE INUIT - also referred to by archaeologists as Thule Eskimo - were the last migrants from Alaska into the Canadian Arctic, and their culture eventually spanned the entire continent from the Bering Sea to Greenland. Around A.D. 1200 they moved southward in the eastern Arctic (possibly because of a deterioration in the northern climate) and are thought to have crossed to Labrador from the east coast of Baffin Island. They arrived in Saglek Bay around A.D. 1500.

The Inuit belonged to a different cultural tradition from the Dorset people, one which featured whale hunting, the use of larger open-water boats as well as kayaks, and the use of dogsleds for hunting animals. For whatever reason, they flourished in the eastern Arctic as the Dorset declined, and they either assimilated or exterminated the older culture as they advanced. We may gather something of the efficiency and daring of the Inuit, as well as their interest in trading with a new people, from the accounts of Martin Frobisher's experiences in Baffin Island in the 1570s.

The Inuit dominated the northern coastline of Labrador, venturing into the southern parts of the region to trade with the Basques and other European seafarers. Their surviving artifacts show evidence of early contact with European technology and quick adaptation to changing conditions.

BRITISH MUSEUM

NFLD. MUSEUM/JACK MARTIN

This famous drawing is by the English artist John White, the first European to draw Canadian Inuit. White may have accompanied Frobisher on his second voyage to South Baffin Island in 1577. His pen and water-colour drawing is of the violent encounter which marred Frobisher's expedition.

In its unusual clarity and immediacy, it must have had a striking impact in the England of his day.

This Inuit wooden man was found by archaeologist Peter Schledermann in Ikkusik, north Labrador. It is a contact piece, dating possibly from the early 1500s, and similar artifacts have been located as far north as Ellesmere Island. Schledermann studied at Memorial University of Newfoundland and is now director of the Arctic Institute of North America, in Calgary. He has been in the forefront of the study, through archaeology, of the earliest links between European and Eskimo cultures.

The Naskapi-Montagnais

LITTLE IS KNOWN about the prehistory of the Naskapi-Montagnais of Labrador, though one archaeologist has suggested that traces of their culture may be as old as A.D. 600. If such traces are indeed to be related to the historic Naskapis, then these Indians once had settlements on the coast. In time, however, they came to dwell only in the forbidding interior of Labrador, where they lived by hunting caribou and other animals. Perhaps they had been driven from the coastline by the more aggressive Eskimo peoples.

Artifacts such as stone tools from the sites of the prehistoric Naskapi suggest a simple culture, though knowledge in this area is imperfect. More recent items, however, reveal a marked flair for intricate and appealing decoration.

This pair of child's caribou-hide boots dates from c.1920. They are suggestive of the long history of the Naskapi-Montagnais as hunters of caribou on the Labrador plateau, and they hint at a culture which accented artistic creativity as well as survival skills.

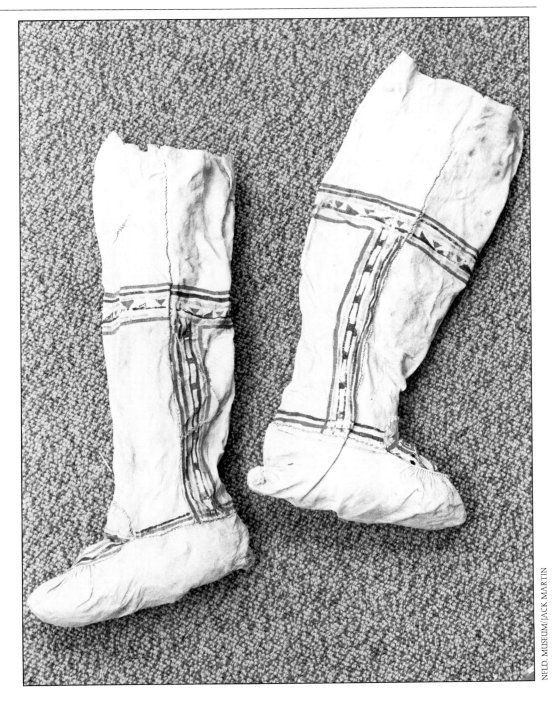

The Beothucks

IT IS PROBABLE that the Beothuck Indians of the island of Newfoundland were descendants of the ancient Maritime Archaic people. They seem to have resembled the earlier people physically, and there were other points of likeness between the two races as well; for example, their common use of red ochre in burials. Moreover, recent archaeological excavation at Cape Freels shows that the Beothucks were living in coastal Newfoundland from A.D. 200 to 750. Thus, somewhat surprisingly, they co-existed for about four centuries with the Dorset Eskimo culture; and there may in fact have been continuous Indian occupation of the island from the time of the earliest primitive settlers.

The Beothucks developed a way of life finely adapted to the Newfoundland environment, moving to and from the sea coast as seasonal changes made different supplies of food available. In the main, they inhabited the coastline and lived on the resources of the sea and seashore: fish, seals, and birds. They may even have ventured fifty kilometres across open ocean to Funk Island in order to kill birds and collect eggs. But in winter they moved inland to hunt caribou, which they smoked to preserve. During the cold season they lived in large groups in big log houses, which were multi-sided at the base and peaked with a conical arrangement of poles covered with birch-bark and moss. By contrast, their moveable summer dwellings were flimsy structures of poles covered with skins or bark. The precarious nature of their life probably ensured that the population of the Beothuck tribe remained small; yet they seem to have been skilled hunters with the bow and arrow, the spear, and the harpoon.

Beothucks made extensive use of birch-bark, not only in building houses and canoes but also in their artwork. Toy birch-bark canoes and skin moccasins were placed in the graves of children. Bone artifacts, used as decorations on their caribou-skin clothing, were also carefully crafted. We know little of their religious beliefs.

Perhaps it was a group of Beothucks, around A.D. 1000, that saw a strange ship appear in a northern bay of what had become their exclusive domain. Their visitors were Norsemen. Although transitory, the first contact had been made in Newfoundland between the European and Amerindian cultures. It was a fateful moment in human history.

Beothuck moccasin. Beothuck burial sites were the subject of some looting in the nineteenth century, since they did not present the same difficulty of access as the remains of earlier peoples. There was, however, a modest amount of systematic collecting of artifacts and some formal study of the Indians. One interested amateur was Samuel Coffin, who about 1875 found Indian implements while clearing land at Long Island, Placentia Bay. In 1886 Coffin acquired more remains from the burial site of a Beothuck child on Burnt Island, Pilley's Tickle, Notre Dame Bay. The site had been discovered accidentally by berry pickers and was one of the most elaborate ever found. According to Coffin, "the body was lying on its left side, enshrouded in a skin covering...the flesh side turned out and smeared with red ochre." Several pairs of moccasins were found, sewn with finely stitched deer sinew.

NFLD. MUSEUM/JACK MARTIN

The Vikings

DURING THE NINTH CENTURY the Norse, in their long ships, headed into the western ocean in search of plunder and new territory. In 870 Iceland was settled; in 986 Eric the Red colonized Greenland. The Vikings were now close to North America - in fact, Cape Bauld on the tip of Newfoundland's Great Northern Peninsula is only about twelve hundred kilometres from southern Greenland, not a great distance for a seafaring people.

In the same year that Greenland was colonized, Bjarni Herjolfson sailed from Norway to join his father in Iceland, but on arriving learned that his father had gone with Eric. Although he did not know how to navigate from Iceland to Greenland, Bjarni decided to take a chance and follow his father. After three days of fair sailing, his ship was blown off course for many days by a northerly wind, so that the crew "had no idea what their course was." When wind and fog subsided, they again hoisted sail and in another day sighted land. It was "not mountainous but was well wooded and with low hills."

This was the country which Leif the Lucky visited around the year 1000. Stepping from their ship after a dangerous voyage, his men put their hands into the grass to collect the dew, then put it to their lips. "To them," it is recorded, "it seemed the sweetest thing they had ever tasted." Leif called the new land Vinland. Here the Norsemen would later try to establish a

The ninth-century Gokstad ship shown here typifies the small craft on which the Vikings ventured onto the North Atlantic. It was excavated in 1881 at Gokstad, near Oslo, Norway. Because of the particular soil in which the ship had been buried, both it and its contents were found in nearly perfect condition; only the posts at the bow and stern had deteriorated over time. The ship had been used to bury some eminent personage, and a chamber had been built on it to contain the remains.

The ship was 23.3 metres long and 5.3 metres wide. The rudder and mast were made of oak. Although designed as a sailing vessel, sixteen pairs of pine oars could be accommodated, and it has been estimated that the full crew on long ocean voyages was about thirty-five men.

In 1893 a replica of the Gokstad ship commanded by Magnus Anderson sailed from Norway to Newfoundland in under a month through rough spring weather.

permanent colony. Bjarni and his men, the first Europeans to see North America, had not landed but had followed a northerly course along Labrador and Baffin Island, then eastward to Greenland. The Vikings knew this southwest route to Vinland for about a hundred years, but by the twelfth century it seems to have been forgotten.

Vinland, described in such detail in the Norse Sagas, was probably located near the present settlement of L'Anse au Meadows in Épaves Bay, near Cape Bauld. The site was discovered in 1960; and excavations between 1961 and 1968 disclosed an elaborate Norse colony, dating from around 1000. The settlement comprised eight buildings of sod and wood: four workshops, three large dwellings which could each house twenty people, and a smithy, all built in the style of contemporary Scandinavian structures. The smithy was used for smelting iron. The discovery at the site of a Viking spindle-whorl, a bronze pin of Viking type, and other artifacts, decisively prove the settlement to have been Norse. The spindle-whorl strongly suggests the presence of women, an indication corroborated by the Sagas. As a fully authenticated Viking settlement site, L'Anse au Meadows is unique in North America and has been declared by UNESCO a World Heritage Site.

According to the Sagas, it was Thorfinn Karlsefni who made the most determined attempt to colonize Vinland, taking with him from Greenland one hundred and sixty men and women, together with live-

L'Anse au Meadows. Leif's voyage of discovery took him first to what he called Helluland ("slab-land"), possibly Baffin Island; then to Markland ("forest-land"), probably Labrador; and finally to Vinland. The voyage from Markland to Vinland took two days. Leif's first landing was on an island; from there he proceeded to the mainland, where his ship, at low tide, was grounded. The Vikings ran ashore to the site of a river; on a rising tide, they took their ship upriver and anchored in a lake, and then established themselves on shore.

Although the description thus given in the Sagas is somewhat elusive, this site was probably Épaves Bay, on which L'Anse au Meadows is located.

According to the Sagas, the name Vinland derives from an incident involving Leif and a "Southerner" named Tyrkir, who claimed to have discovered grapes and vines, which he recognized from his birthplace. On hearing this, Leif set out to obtain a cargo of wood, grapes, and vines. The grapes collected are said to have filled a tow boat. Hence the name Vinland.

What did Leif see? The Great Northern Peninsula, where Épaves Bay is located, abounds in squash-berries and other wild fruit such as blueberries, depicted here. Leif may have talked about grapes for the same reason that Eric the Red called another island Greenland – to attract others to the land he had discovered.

stock. The attempt was abandoned after three winters, partly owing to the hostility of the natives of the area, whom the Norse derisively called Skraelings ("wretches"). Although Thorfinn's colonists managed for a while to trade with these Skraelings, amicable relations eventually broke down, and the first attempts at founding a European colony in the New World ended in bloodshed and failure.

This plaque was unveiled by the Hon. John Roberts in July 1980. L'Anse au Meadows is one of four sites in Canada on the World Heritage list.

AT THE 1978 MEETING OF THE WORLD HERITAGE COMMITTEE ESTABLISHED UNDER THE UNESCO WORLD HERITAGE CONVENTION. L'ANSE AUX MEADOWS NATIONAL HISTORIC PARK WAS NOMINATED TO THE WORLD HERITAGE LIST AS AN OUTSTANDING CULTURAL SITE FORMING PART OF THE HERITAGE OF MANKIND.

L'ANSE AUX MEADOWS IS THE FIRST AUTHENTICATED NORSE SITE IN NORTH AMERICA. ITS SOD BUILDINGS ARE THUS THE EARLIEST KNOWN EUROPEAN STRUCTURES ON THIS CONTINENT; ITS SMITHY THE SITE OF THE FIRST KNOWN IRON WORKING IN THE NEW WORLD; THE SITE ITSELF THE SCENE OF THE FIRST CONTACTS BETWEEN NATIVE AMERICANS AND EUROPEANS. IT IS THEREFORE ONE OF THE WORLD'S MAJOR ARCHAEOLOGICAL SITES.

PARKS CANADA

PARKS CANADA

In 1953 the Norwegian archaeologist Helge Ingstad (left) journeyed to Greenland to study Norse settlement. On the basis of his experiences there, he theorized that the site of Vinland was farther north than was generally believed at the time. His ideas were similar to those of an early Newfoundland student of the question, W. A. Munn, and the Finnish archaeologist V. Tanner.

Acting on his beliefs, Ingstad proceeded to Newfoundland in 1960, eventually coming to L'Anse au Meadows on the Grenfell mission ship *Albert T. Gould*. There he met George Decker, inquired about "ruins" in the area, and was told that "something like that" existed at nearby Black Duck Brook. When Ingstad saw the brook and its environs, geography and literary knowledge combined in his mind and led him to one of the greatest of modern archaeological discoveries.

In 1968, following early archaeological excavation, the Government of Canada declared the L'Anse au Meadows site to be of national historic significance. Two years later, an international research advisory committee, including scholars from Scandinavia, Iceland, and Canada, was formed to give direction on further study and conservation. Parks Canada carried out its own excavation beginning in 1973, and in 1977 the site was designated a national historic park. As shown here, the buildings have been reconstructed in authentic Norse fashion.

PARKS CANADA

"A Very Wildernesse"

SOME FIVE CENTURIES after the Norse attempt at colonization near L'Anse au Meadows, Europeans rediscovered the island of Newfoundland. On June 24, 1497, John Cabot, a Venetian citizen acting under authority granted in letters patent issued by Henry VII of England, stepped ashore in the New World and, according to one account, "raised banners with the arms of the Holy Father and those of the King." Many believe this initial landing to have been on the island of Newfoundland. On his return to England in August, news of his voyage spread quickly throughout the courts on the continent. One report to the Duke of Milan a few months after the voyage quoted Cabot's opinion that "the sea there is swarming with fish, which can be taken not only with the net, but in baskets let down with a stone." The curiosity and greed of all Europe were stirred by such stories. But men thought of more than codfish; they dreamed of gold, silver, and diamonds.

In Cabot's wake came Portuguese, Spanish, and French adventurers. Gaspar Corte-Real's expedition of 1501 brought back to Portugal around fifty aborigines from Newfoundland or Labrador (or both) and the promise of many more "men slaves." The land he visited, called "Terra del Rey de Portuguall," is pictured on the Cantino map of 1502 – one of the earliest surviving cartographic representations of Newfoundland. Corte-Real himself was lost on the expedition, and his

According to one source, John Cabot arrived back in Bristol on August 6, 1497, and reported his discovery to the king soon afterwards. The script shown here is taken from the daybooks of the king's payments, dated August 10-11, 1497, and reads as follows: "Item to hym that founde the new Isle - x li" (i.e. £10). This entry is one of the most famous evidences of Cabot's discovery.

This oil painting of Portuguese carracks was executed c. 1535 and is attributed to Cornelis Anthoniszoon. The exploration of the New World was made possible by improvements in ship design and navigation, and the Portuguese were European leaders in seagoing technology. The carrack had been used by Italians in the Mediterranean as early as the thirteenth century and was later modified by the Portuguese for use in northern waters and on longer voyages.

brother Miguel met a similar fate in 1502. Labrador seems to have taken its name from a third Portuguese, João Fernandes, a landholder (or labrador) in the Azores. Yet another Portuguese, João Fagundes, explored the south coast of Newfoundland in 1521. Giovanni da Verrazzano, a Florentine in the service of France, and Estevão Gomes undertook separate voyages in the 1520s and helped to define the coastline of North America. Both were trying to find a westerly sea route to China and the East Indies – an objective pursued earlier through more northern waters by John Cabot's son, Sebastian. Perhaps the most important voyages in Newfoundland waters in the first half of the century were those of Jacques Cartier. On his route westward to the Gulf of St. Lawrence in 1534, Cartier

explored Funk Island, part of the Labrador coast, and the west coast of Newfoundland, distributing French names liberally as he travelled.

While this quixotic exploration was proceeding, a variety of national groups were carrying on the more mundane but in fact more lucrative business of fishing. It is surprising how quickly European fishermen were able to cash in on Cabot's discoveries. Although the English fishery remained focused on the waters near Iceland for the first half of the century, the Portuguese and French, followed shortly by the Spanish, moved swiftly to exploit the fishery to the west. For much of the sixteenth century, the Newfondland fishery was in effect an international resource, exploited by various competing yet often peaceably co-existing European

---

This is a detail by the historian Henry Harrisse from the Cantino world map of 1502, which is believed to have incorporated, for the first time, information from the voyages of Gaspar Corte-Real. This island was marked on the map as "Terra del Rey de Portuguall" ("land of the king of Portugal"). Note the indented seacoast, which resembles the northeast coastline of Newfoundland; the Portuguese were enormously impressed by the forests they saw.

Sebastian Cabot was the son of John Cabot and like his father was referred to as a Venetian. He is thought to have undertaken a journey westward in 1508 or 1509, his object, according to one contemporary, being to find a northern passage to Cathay. He explored coasts which he apparently called the "Bachalaos" ("codfish") and may have approached Hudson Bay. This portrait shows him in his old age.

The impact of discovery upon the British imagination was evident from the early sixteenth century. The Scot William Dunbar alludes to the "new fund Yle" in this poem written c. 1503, entitled "Of the Warldis Instabilitie" This extract from the poem is taken from the ancient Maitland Folio Manuscript in Magdalene College, Cambridge. Complaining about how long it is taking him to get a benefice, he says: "It micht have cuming in schortar quhyll/Fra Calyecot and the new fund Yle/The partis of Transmeridiane/Quhilk to considder is ane pane." (The Portuguese Vasco da Gama had reached Calicut on the Malabar coast of India in 1498.) In a dramatic work called *Hyckescorner*, published c. 1510 and here also illustrated, a character actually claims to have travelled in the newly discovered island, presumably Newfoundland. Print and discovery, emblems of the new age, were united.

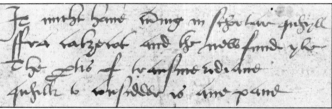

interests. When the Englishman John Rut visited St. John's in 1527, for example, he counted fourteen ships from Normandy, Brittany and Portugal, "all a fishing." Nor was cod the only species taken. In the middle decades of the century the Basques developed an extensive and profitable whaling industry on the coast of Labrador.

By the 1570s English interest in the Newfoundland fishery was beginning to grow. A new "dry" method of curing fish was apparently making a distant migratory fishery more attractive, and markets for the English were opening up in the Mediterranean. Anthony Parkhurst, a merchant who fished successfully in Newfoundland in 1575-77, actually suggested that the English colonize the island. Occupation of the Strait of Belle Isle, he said, would make the English masters of the European fishermen in the area. His views may have influenced Humphrey Gilbert, whose elaborate plans for a colony in the New World came to grief following what was intended to be a stopover in Newfoundland in 1583. On entering St. John's harbour in August, he found no fewer than thirty-six fishing ships, sixteen of which were English. He took formal possession of the island on August 5. So impressed was Gilbert with the fancied resources of Newfoundland – including silver – that he declared he had become "a Northerne man altogether." The Hungarian poet Stephen Parmenius, who had unluckily accompanied Gilbert on his expedition, had a different view. "What shall I say," he wrote from St. John's to his friend Richard Hakluyt in England, "when I see nothing but a very wildernesse?"

This ship, sailing to the west, and represented on Pierre Descelliers's map of the known world, c. 1546, may well have resembled Cartier's.

Jacques Cartier was born in St. Malo, Brittany, c. 1491, and died there in 1557. He may have been with Verrazzano on his 1524 expedition, which touched Newfoundland. The formal objective of Cartier's 1534 voyage was "to discover certain islands and lands where it is said that a great quantity of gold, and other precious things, are to be found." He commanded on this mission two ships and sixty-one men, leaving St. Malo on April 20. This portrait is from a drawing by Théophile Hamel after an original by François Riso.

Funk Island, also known as The Funks, lies 50 kilometres north-northeast of the north bill of Cape Freels. A barren, primeval rock, difficult of access, it is the habitat of innumerable puffins, gannets, and other sea birds. With one of Newfoundland's most celebrated place names and an enduring symbol of wildness and remoteness, Funk Island evokes the same awe in modern man that it evoked in Cartier in 1534.

The most amazing sight that greeted Cartier at Funk Island was the great auk, a flightless bird which became extinct in 1844. Cartier wrote that these birds were "as large as geese, being black and white with a beak like a crow's. They are always in the water, not being able to fly in the air, inasmuch as they have only small wings about the size of half one's hand, with which however they move as quickly along the water as the other birds fly through the air. And these birds are so fat that it is marvellous....Our two long-boats were laden with them as with stones, in less than half an hour."

The specimen illustrated is the only one in Canada. It was once owned by John James Audubon and was acquired by the Royal Ontario Museum in 1965.

This coastline typifies what Cartier may have seen in the region of the Strait of Belle Isle.

Cartier was shocked by the bleakness of the Great Northern Peninsula and the southern coast of Labrador. He stated emphatically that these regions "should not be called the New Land, being composed of stones and horrible rugged rocks." The phrases he used specifically to describe Labrador, in John Florio's translation of 1580, convey his dismay: "There is nothing else but Mosse, and small Thornes scattered here and there, withered and drye. To be shorte, I believe that this was the lande that God allotted to Caine."

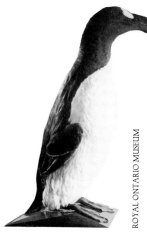

Archaeological work at Red Bay, Labrador, where the Basques had a whaling station in the sixteenth century. In the foreground, archaeologists from Memorial University of Newfoundland can be seen at work on Saddle Island. Offshore, the Parks Canada research barge is located above the underwater remains of the Basque whaling ship, the *San Juan*. In the background can be seen the settlement of Red Bay.

The work at Red Bay has been complemented by major archival discoveries relating to the Basques by Selma Barkham, working in Spain.

Underwater view of the *San Juan*, discovered on the ocean floor in Red Bay in September 1978. She is seen here amidships, with the archaeologists' aluminum grids in place.

Quid Non

Born in 1537, Sir Humphrey Gilbert knew Martin Frobisher and like him was captivated by the idea of finding a northwest passage, an Elizabethan obsession. An initial transatlantic foray in 1578-79 was largely a failure, and Queen Elizabeth was reluctant to send him again, regarding him as "a man noted of not good happ by sea." But she at last consented, sending him "an ancor guyded by a Lady" as a token of her good wishes before his 1583 mission. On this second journey Gilbert commanded five ships, although one, the largest, returned to port soon after departure in June from Plymouth. He was initially bound for Newfoundland, his ultimate destination being the American coast, where he planned to establish "a colonial Utopia" with himself as landlord. The expedition was a disastrous failure, and Gilbert was lost at sea returning from Newfoundland. This portrait, with its motto "Why not?", captures something of the man's cosmopolitan bravado.

The growth of the international fishery in Newfoundland in the sixteenth century is nicely illustrated in this detail from a contemporary map. The map was drawn by the Italian Giacomo Gastaldi and first appeared in a work by the historian G. B. Ramusio in 1556. It may, however, have been engraved earlier. It is called the Gastaldi map. The "Terra Nvova," a variant of which is still applied to Newfoundland, is prominent, as is the name "Terra de Laborador," Cape Bonavista is also identified, and there is an island called "Bacalaos," Portuguese for codfish. A variety of offshore and onshore activities can be seen, and a cross has been placed on the largest of the islands at the bottom of the picture.

Early Settlement

THE WAR WITH SPAIN at the end of the sixteenth century did not prevent the expansion of the English fishing fleet in Newfoundland – it had grown to about one hundred and fifty ships by 1604 – but naturally it deflected attention away from any organized colonial enterprises. When war ended, however, interest in forming colonies revived. Between 1610 and 1661 a number of attempts were made to establish English plantations in Newfoundland. Companies and individuals secured land grants from the crown or from other companies and sent out groups of settlers under a governor to exploit such resources as they could find.

The hope was that settlement would make the fishery more efficient and profitable. But profit was not the sole impulse behind the founding of these colonies; personal ambition, nationalism, and the desire for religious freedom were motives as well.

The first of these plantations was established at Cuper's Cove (now Cupids) in Conception Bay in 1610 under the governorship of John Guy. Guy sailed from Bristol with thirty-nine colonists, arriving in St. John's late in the season, in August. Their first winter was not harsh; yet four of the thirty-nine perished. Guy set about exploring the countryside and searching for minerals. But there were none in the vicinity (he would later be charged with deceiving British investors about the mineral potential of the area). He built houses and

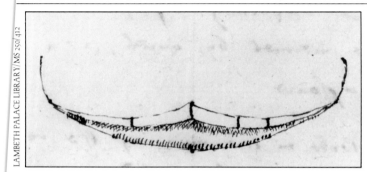

This drawing appears in the manuscript journal of the *Indeavour*, one of the boats in which John Guy and eighteen men left Cupids on October 7, 1612, bound for Trinity Bay. Their purpose was exploration of the coast and communication with the Beothucks. The representation of the canoe shown here is the earliest known authentic European depiction of Beothuck culture.

BELOW
A representation of Guy's encounter with the Beothucks, from Theodor de Bry's *America* pt. XIII, ed. Matthaeus Merian (1634).

cleared land for farming. But while Cuper's Cove was a fine harbour, it was on a coast where agriculture could not prosper. Work on the plantation was grindingly hard, and there were doubts about the fertility of the soil; it was soon learned that grain would not grow there. Even furs were scarce. Before long, there were requests to return home. Slowly the colony faded.

Guy perhaps cannot be faulted for the decline of the plantation. He had a marked capacity as a leader, and his enterprising spirit led him to arrange the only known contact of a friendly nature between Europeans and a group of Beothucks. The encounter, which took place in Bull Arm, Trinity Bay, in 1612, was a poignant and revealing moment in Newfoundland history. When the peaceful intentions of the Euro-peans became clear to the Beothucks, they sang and danced. Among other gifts, Guy gave them "beere and aqua-vitae" to drink, whereupon "one of them, blow-ing in the aqua-vitae bottle, made a sound, which they fell all into laughing at." However, his attempt to establish trade with the Indians came to nothing.

The experience of the English colonists at Cupids was repeated in other plantations on the Avalon Penin-sula, ventures which produced, as an ironic adjunct to failure, a plethora of books advocating settlement and extolling the resources of Newfoundland. In 1626, as the colonies were faltering, one enthusiast described the island as "*Great Britaines Indies*, never to be exhausted dry." Such a contrast between literary exaggeration and stern reality would mark later decades of the

---

Bristol's interest in Newfoundland colonization did not end with Guy's plantation at Cuper's Cove. A new grant of land to merchant venturers in the city led to the establishment of a colony at Bristol's Hope, Conception Bay, c. 1618. One of the governors of this colony was the poet Robert Hayman, a Devonshire man who was in Newfoundland sporadically until 1628, his initial visit apparently lasting fifteen months. In 1628 he published the work illustrated here, the first book of English poetry to be written in what is now Canada.

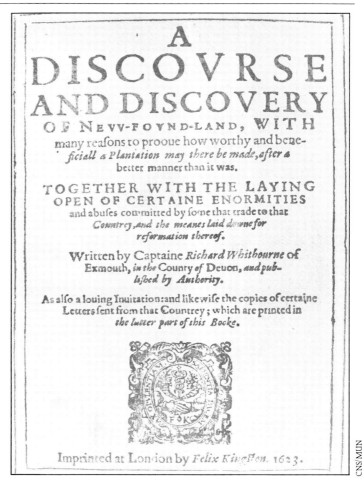

English enthusiasm for Newfoundland settlement in the 1620s found vigorous and diverse literary expression. One of the most notable of the island's publicists was Richard Whitbourne, whose *Discourse and Discovery of Newfoundland* was published initially in 1620 and later reprinted. Whitbourne's writing about Newfoundland was based on first-hand knowledge dating back to 1579.

island's history as well. Pinched and poor as Newfoundland was often destined to become, it rarely lacked the consolation of panegyric. But these early colonies left behind more than empty phrases. A trickle of permanent settlers stayed on along the harsh coastline of Avalon, and by 1660 there was a small resident population in Conception Bay, St. John's, and along the southern shore. Grain and other seeds might not grow, but these took root, the ancient forbears of Newfoundlanders.

By 1660 too, the method of English exploitation of Newfoundland had been established. It was not to be carried out through organized colonies but through the annual migratory fishery in ships from the West Country of England, a system which had improbably succeeded when Cupids had not. The laws by which Newfoundland would be governed for roughly the next century and a half would be determined by powerful fishing interests in England. In their hands the island would long remain, not a colony, but a mere fishing station.

Near the end of Whitbourne's description of Newfoundland, he tells of seeing a mermaid in St. John's harbour. The scene is depicted here, from Theodor de Bry's *America*, pt. XIII, ed. Matthaeus Merian (1628).

George Calvert, later Lord Baltimore, was born in Yorkshire, England, c. 1580, and became a prominent figure at court. In 1620 he acquired land in Newfoundland from Sir William Vaughan and established a settlement at Ferryland on the southern shore in 1621. On April 7, 1623, he obtained a royal charter for the Province of Avalon. Following his conversion to Roman Catholicism, Baltimore visited Newfoundland in 1627, returning there the following year with his family. His experience of Newfoundland during the winter of 1628-29 gave the lie to optimistic literary reports, and Baltimore thereafter shifted the focus of his colonizing efforts to a more temperate clime, promoting the settlement of Maryland.

This extract from a letter written by Baltimore on August 18, 1629, to Sir Francis Cottington graphically conveys his shocked reaction to his first and only winter in Newfoundland. He writes of his wife and children here: "I have sent them home after much sufferance in this wofull country, where with one intolerable wynter were we almost undone. It is not to be expressed with my pen what wee have endured."

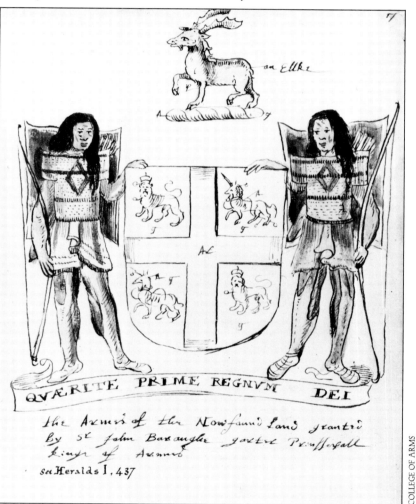

This coat of arms was assigned by the Garter Principal King of Arms on January 1, 1638, following the granting of the whole of Newfoundland to the Marquis of Hamilton, the Earl of Pembroke, the Earl of Holland, and Sir David Kirke. The crest is an elk, an animal erroneously believed to inhabit Newfoundland. The arms consist of a silver cross set on a red field, the quarters featuring lions and unicorns. The arms are supported on each side by "a savage of the area armed and habited as for war." They show therefore what the designer thought the Beothucks looked like. The motto "Quaerite prime regnum Dei" ("Seek ye first the kingdom of God") is in Matthew, 7, 23. The existence of this coat of arms was in time forgotten. Uncovered in the 1920s, it was officially adopted by Newfoundland.

An eighteenth-century view
(with explanatory diagram) of
Benjamin Lester's fishing
establishment at Trinity,
Trinity Bay. The Lesters were
one of the great merchant
families of Poole, Dorset,
an English port with a rich
Newfoundland connection.

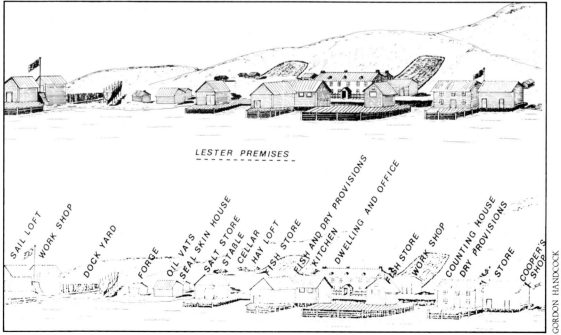

LESTER PREMISES

SAIL LOFT · WORK SHOP · DOCK YARD · FORGE · OIL VATS · SEAL SKIN HOUSE · SALT STORE · STABLE · CELLAR · HAY LOFT · FISH STORE · FISH AND DRY PROVISIONS · KITCHEN · DWELLING AND OFFICE · FISH STORE · WORK SHOP · COUNTING HOUSE DRY PROVISIONS · STORE · COOPER'S SHOP

CHAPTER TWO

MORE THAN A FISHERY, LESS THAN A COLONY

DORSET COUNTY MUSEUM

Transatlantic Fishery

As THE EARLY ATTEMPTS TO DEVELOP colonies in Newfoundland failed, official British policy came to favour the claims of West Country migratory fishermen over the rights of any would-be or actual settlers on the island. The Western Charter of 1634 appeared to place authority in each harbour in the hands of the first ship's captain who arrived from England in the spring. The charter called him "Admirall of the said Harbour," though in fact no legal power was given to him. Additional regulations in 1671 specified that "no planter should cut down any wood, or should plant within six miles of the sea" and that "no seaman or fisherman should remain behind, after the fishing was ended." Such measures were not rigidly enforced, despite some inevitable friction between the settlers and visiting fishermen. James Yonge's account of his experiences with migratory fishing crews in 1663-70 refers to "planters," "inhabitants," and - a suggestive word - "interlopers"; but the scenes evoked by him are peaceful. Moreover, the *English Pilot*'s 1689 map of St. John's harbour shows that the resident planters had fishing rooms there.

In the closing decades of the seventeenth century the policy of the British government towards Newfoundland wavered between prohibiting and allowing settlement. In 1699 the policy was at last clarified by the passing of King William's Act, which in effect permitted limited settlement but withheld year-round residential law and government. The intention seems to have been to keep the fishery the preserve of the West Country, and yet, by allowing scattered settlement, to maintain the English hold on the island against any possible move by the French. At the same time, the few settlers who would choose to live in a place without continuous civil government would hardly interfere with the fishermen from Poole, Plymouth, and other West Country ports, and might even aid their enterprise. It was a policy which ensured that

Newfoundland would not develop as a normal colony. Newfoundland in the late seventeenth and eighteenth centuries was indeed a source of wealth and influence, but to the merchants of the west of England rather than to the people of the island. Whole towns in the West Country were dependent on the trade; reputations, fortunes, country estates, and even political careers were built on the humble cod.

The early English fishery was carried out mainly on Newfoundland's east coast, with the French bank fishery centred in the south, where France's claims were reinforced by the fortification of Placentia (Plaisance) in 1662. In the eighteenth century, however, the English moved into the south and north coastlines of the island, and across to Labrador. As the century progressed, the nature of the English fishery changed. The shore-based migratory ship fishery declined and by the 1780s had virtually disappeared. In its place there developed an offshore bank fishery carried out from eastern harbours, supplemented by the inshore activities of smaller operators known as byeboat fishermen, who were a transitional phase between the old ship fishery and that of the emerging resident planters and their servants. By the end of the eighteenth century, the byeboat fishery too had faded.

During the eighteenth century the big merchants diversified into shipbuilding, trapping, seal hunting, and trading in merchandise. As the role of the great mercantile families such as the Slades of Twillingate and the Lesters of Trinity changed, their establishments in Newfoundland became more elaborate, little resembling, however, the mansions and town houses waiting for them at home in England.

Philip Henry Gosse's drawing of the codfish, the basis of Newfoundland's transatlantic economy.

The drawing of a fishing premises is taken from the journal of James Yonge, who first visited Newfoundland in 1663, working as a ship's surgeon. His account of his Newfoundland experiences is a rich source for understanding the practices of the migratory fishery. The drawing shows a stage, stage head, fishing boat, cook room, and flake for drying fish – essential and enduring components of the Newfoundland fishery.

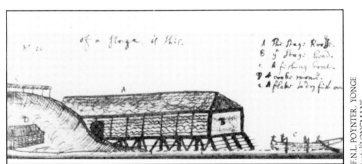

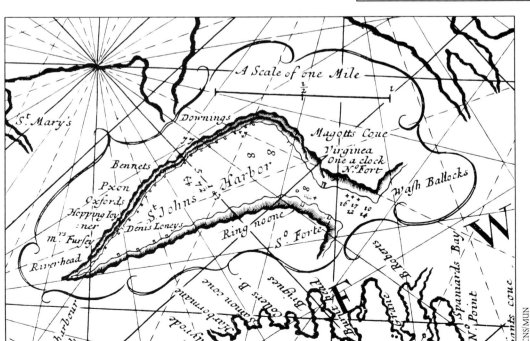

This inset from the *English Pilot* of 1689 shows that by this date St. John's was being used by both migratory fishermen and resident planters. Tiny white squares indicate planters' fishing rooms and tiny black squares those reserved for the ship fishermen from overseas. The names of planters are also listed.

Arthur Holdsworth was admiral of St. John's harbour in 1700 and in other years around the turn of the century. He was born in Dartmouth in 1668, the son of a vicar from a Yorkshire family who had married a Newman, a great name in the Newfoundland trade. Holdsworth was known for bringing passengers to Newfoundland in the spring and leaving them behind in the ensuing winter – thus was settlement built up on the island. In 1697 he took the 250 ton *Nicholas* from Dartmouth to Newfoundland with one hundred passengers who were returning to the island after a year's disruption of their residence overseas caused by the French. To these people, Newfoundland was apparently home. Holdsworth was one of a line of five in the family with the same name, most of them prominent in the fishery to Newfoundland. He died in 1726 while mayor of Dartmouth. The Holdsworths became important merchants and landowners in eighteenth century Devonshire.

One of the great centres of the migratory English fishery was Trinity, Trinity Bay. This plan, dated 1700, is the earliest known depiction of a fishing room at this location. The premises shown belonged to William Taverner. A large flake can be seen in the upper right, a smaller one to the left of the picture. The small buildings labelled N, M, and L are fishing houses near the landwash. The owner's house is marked P. The clearly designated uneven line is a path which passes under both flakes. The stage is marked Q.

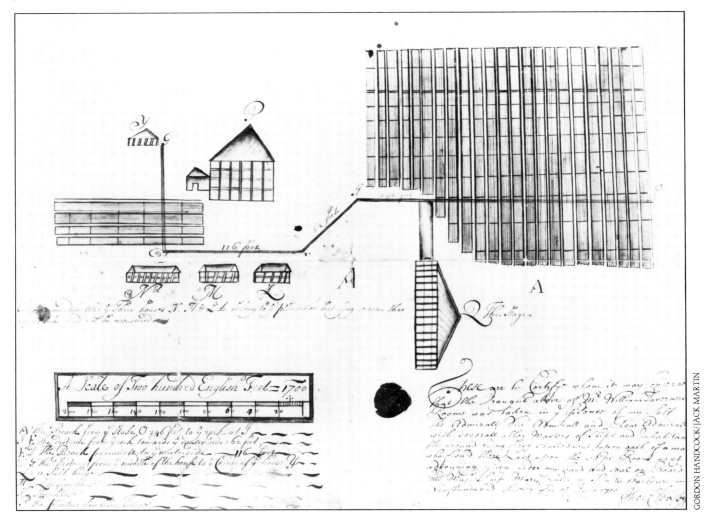

Widdecombe House near Dartmouth, Devon, built in the early eighteenth century, typifies the affluence created in Devonshire and neighbouring English counties on the proceeds of the Newfoundland trade. It is associated with the Holdsworth family. Now owned by a Newman, it was used during World War II by General Dwight D. Eisenhower, its library becoming his map room.

GORDON HANDCOCK

Another eighteenth-century painting of Benjamin Lester's establishment at Trinity. Many of the activities of the fishery are depicted here. Fish are being dried on the flake in the foreground. The rich history of Trinity has been skilfully explored by the historical geographer Gordon Handcock.

DORSET COUNTY MUSEUM

Amy Garland, daughter of Benjamin Lester, was born at Trinity in 1759. She married George Garland and bore him eight sons and two daughters. She died in 1819.

George Garland was from another leading Poole mercantile family whose wealth was founded on Newfoundland. He was M.P. for Poole from 1801 to 1806. He was also a magistrate, and served as Mayor of Poole in 1788 and 1810. He died in 1825.

The French bank fishery. At the top is a French ship at sea, its operations revealed. The man below deck is a salter. The closer view of the work shows: on the left, a header; in the middle, a cutter; and at right, a man fishing.

The stone cottage of George and Amy Garland at Wimborne Minster, Dorset, England.

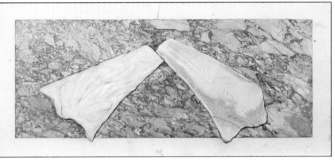

Dried cod, in marble, over the fireplace in the Mansion House, Poole. Started by Isaac Lester in 1776 and completed by his son Benjamin, this house is one of the most famous in this part of England. Beneath the grandeur of the upper floors, there was in Benjamin Lester's day a basement counting house, full of busy clerks. The house is used now as a hotel and dining club. Its fireplace symbolizes Newfoundland's West Country roots.

Conflict and Diplomacy

IN THE LATE SEVENTEENTH and eighteenth centuries the squalid conflicts in the bone heap of Europe reverberated in Newfoundland, which became a theatre of war and a prize over which European diplomats bargained. The Dutch under Lieutenant Admiral Michiel De Ruyter attacked St. John's in 1665, but were so struck by the poverty of the inhabitants that they did not burn the settlement. The Dutch also raided Ferryland in 1673.

But it was the French whose ambition and armies gave most anxiety. In 1696-97 the French Canadian adventurer Pierre Le Moyne d'Iberville took St. John's and pillaged the small English coastal fishing settlements that had been struggling for survival on the Avalon Peninsula. In four months the French destroyed thirty-six settlements, killing two hundred people and taking seven hundred prisoners. Immediately after the Canadians' departure, however, English troops landed in St. John's, and normal life of a sort resumed in the colony.

Precious little in the way of strategic advantage had been gained by d'Iberville's raid, but the French were back again in 1705 to destroy more settlements, this time using Micmac Indians (who had come to Newfoundland because of a shortage of game in Cape Breton) to terrorize the shore from Renews to Bonavista. Then, in 1708, the French took the newly

A French map of Placentia from Baron Lahontan's *Voyages* (1706). The original fortifications were built near sea level, but in 1692 construction was started on Castle Hill, and Fort Royal was begun there in 1693. By the early years of the new century, the French were well entrenched on a strategic site.

Portrait of Lieutenant Admiral Michiel Adriaenszoon De Ruyter (1607-76), commander of the Dutch forces in Newfoundland waters in 1665. He is shown here on a medal struck after the famous "Four Days' Fight," June 1-4, 1666, in the second Anglo-Dutch War. The obverse of the medal shows Dutch warships at sea.

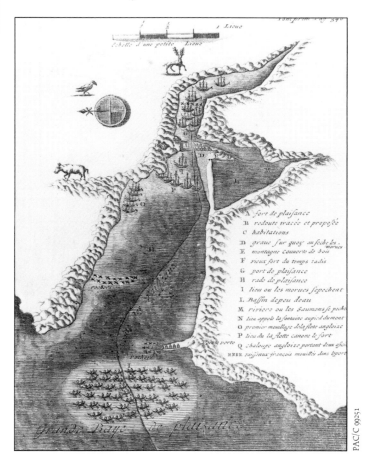

built Fort William in St. John's. But although they won in Newfoundland, they lost overall in the war against England; and in the Treaty of Utrecht (1713) France gave up her claims to Newfoundland. The French had to vacate Placentia, but they retained rights to catch, land, and dry fish on the north and west coastline between Cape Bonavista and Point Riche. This was the so-called French Shore (or Treaty Shore).

In June 1762, during the Seven Years' War, St. John's again fell to the French, though William Amherst retook it for the English in September. According to the naturalist Sir Joseph Banks, writing in 1766, the "Irish and fishermen" in St. John's had gone over to the French "as soon as ever they saw them." At the end of the war, under the terms of the Treaty of Paris (1763),

the French handed over Labrador to England but retained their rights to the French Shore. The islands of St. Pierre and Miquelon were now also ceded to France. Then, in 1783, the Treaty of Versailles altered the limits of the French Shore: henceforth it ran from Cape St.John to Cape Ray. Thus, despite great military defeats, France had retained important bases of operation for her fishery in the North Atlantic; although she lost the wars, she did not lose everything in the treaties.

The Treaty of Versailles also gave Americans extensive fishing and landing liberties in Newfoundland and Labrador. But by the Anglo-American Convention of 1818, following the War of 1812, their fishing liberties

New France's greatest soldier, Pierre Le Moyne d'Iberville was born at Ville-Marie (Montreal). His career carried him over vast distances, and his mode of warfare was fierce and well suited to North American conditions. This was exemplified by his expedition to Newfoundland, when he led

a small troop overland from Placentia to St. John's, sweeping all before him in the face of bleak winter conditions. He died in 1706 and is buried in Havana, Cuba.

A French representation of the military events of 1696 in Newfoundland.

Les Anglois chassez de leurs habitations de Terre-neuve par les Francois au Mois de 7bre et d'Octobre 1696.

BIBLIOTHÈQUE NATIONALE/PAC/C84899

PAC/C 20026

The French capture of St. John's in 1762 inspired this vignette, executed, with an inscription, at Basset's, Rue St. Jacques, Paris. The scene is more a patriotic statement than a realistic depiction of what happened. Certainly, the topography bears little resemblance to St. John's and its environs.

PAC/C 40901

were scaled down to two specific areas: from the Quirpon to the Ramea islands on the north, west, and south coasts of the island; and, in Labrador, from Mount Joly northward. American landing rights were further confined to the south coast of Newfoundland from Cape Ray to the Ramea islands and to the Labrador coast.

This view of the harbour at St. Pierre, one of the islands ceded to France in 1763, is taken from Jean Dominique Cassini's *Voyage fait par ordre du roi en 1768* (Paris, 1770). It suggests the potential of St. Pierre as a base for France's North Atlantic fishery.

Lieutenant-Colonel William Amherst, who recaptured St. John's from the French in 1762. The portrait is by Robert Edge Pine. Amherst's troops landed at Torbay and marched to Quidi Vidi. From there his men forced the French back towards Signal Hill, and after capturing it, successfully attacked Fort William. Seven hundred and seventy prisoners were taken by Amherst, though the French fleet was able to escape by night. It was thus in St. John's that the French flag of empire was pulled down for the last time in what is now Canada.

This eighteenth-century English map of Newfoundland includes the designated limits of the French Shore, as specified in 1713 and 1783: Cape Bonavista, Cape John, Point Riche, and Cape Ray. St. Pierre is shown as St. Peter's Island.

A View of the Town

After recapturing St. John's in 1762, Great Britain decided that more fortifications were needed there. A new fort was completed in 1777. Named Fort Townshend in honour of George Townshend, master general of the Board of Ordnance, it is clearly visible in this picture, dominating the landscape, an emblem of British hegemony over the island of Newfoundland.

An American brig in Trepassey harbour, July 4, 1786. Its presence in Newfoundland on a symbolic day is indicative of the American interest in the fisheries of the region.

Naval Ascendancy

IN 1689 THE BRITISH GOVERNMENT ordered that "a Governor be forthwith sent to Newfoundland"; but the decision, perhaps made as a worried response to the growth of the French settlement at Placentia, was not acted upon. Ten years later King William's Act made the commander of the naval convoy, which annually accompanied the fishing fleet, in effect an appeal judge to whom inhabitants and ships' masters could refer disputes with the admirals of the harbours. Thus the naval commodore became a kind of governor, though it was not until 1729, after a period of "great disorders" and "anarchy" in the colony, that he was formally made Governor and Commander-in-Chief in Newfoundland. Typically, changes in British administration had come about only when the utter inadequacy of existing arrangements had been demonstrated; there was no foresight or planning, only distant tinkering with an antique system – government after the event.

After 1729 the government of Newfoundland became a function of the British navy. Naval commanders arrived with their entourages in summer, presided briefly, and departed in the fall, their labours over. This bizarre system of administration endured until 1817. The governors' sway in distant harbours was enforced by surrogates, or subordinate naval officers, who went to the larger outports to uphold justice as

A pencil drawing of Sir Joseph Banks by Henry Edridge. A great naturalist, Banks came to Newfoundland in 1766 at the beginning of his long scientific career. He enjoyed the favour of Palliser and while in St. John's attended a ball given by the governor to celebrate the coronation of George III. Banks was a keen observer of Newfoundland life and may be said to have started the scientific study of the island's plant kingdom.

Sir Hugh Palliser, by George Dance. This energetic governor first arrived in Newfoundland waters the day after the surrender of the French forces in 1762. He was named governor in 1764. In this office, which he held until 1768, he implemented an aggressive new British policy in Newfoundland and visited the coast of Labrador, which had been placed under the authority of the governor of Newfoundland in 1763. His ambition for Labrador was that the English migratory fishery should be extended to it. Palliser also went to the French Shore and took steps to keep the French within their treaty limits. And he encouraged the mapping of Newfoundland by his fellow naval officer, James Cook. Palliser's policies in Newfoundland reflected Britain's growing realization of the importance of the Newfoundland fishery.

Specimens of *Potentilla nivea* collected by Joseph Banks on a dry hillside at Conche, Newfoundland, in 1766. Banks sailed along the Newfoundland coast on H.M.S. *Niger*.

NEWFOUNDLAND. BANKS. 1766.

well as they could. These surrogate courts were still in session as late as 1825.

The improvement or damage that a naval governor caused in Newfoundland depended, in part, on the individual's personality and ambitions. But it was not to be expected that such men – who were merely the instruments of a half-forgotten colonial policy and more accustomed to the rough justice of a quarterdeck than to constitutional niceties – would become social and administrative innovators. Yet it was during the regime of the naval governors that the scientific mapping and study of Newfoundland were commenced, exploration of the interior was encouraged, Labrador was opened up to English enterprise, and efforts were made to protect the dwindling Beothuck population.

James Cook (1728-79), by Nathaniel Dance. One of the most famous officers in British naval history, Cook first came to Newfoundland in 1763, surveying St. Pierre and Miquelon, and certain northern harbours during this first summer there. He returned every summer until 1767, and when he had finished his work, navigation in Newfoundland had been greatly advanced, thanks to his skilful mapping.

Born in Nottinghamshire in 1739, George Cartwright entered the army and rose to the brevet rank of captain. Leaving his military career behind, he established himself in 1770 at Charles Harbour, Labrador, becoming the second English planter to attempt a living there. He trapped, fished, hunted, and traded for sixteen years at this site and farther north in Sandwich Bay. He left an account of his experiences in a classic *Journal*, published in 1792, of which this portrait is the frontispiece.

In 1772 five Inuit were taken to England by George Cartwright. One of them, a man named Attuiock, is shown here in a portrait by Nathaniel Dance. Attuiock and three of his companions died of smallpox and never again saw Labrador.

Portrait of Caubvick by Nathaniel Dance. She was the only member of Cartwright's party of Inuit to survive the trip to England. She was, however, greatly disfigured by smallpox and lost her husband, Tooklavinia, who also made the journey.

In August 1768 the naval officer Lieutenant John Cartwright, George Cartwright's brother, led a small party up the Exploits River into the interior of Newfoundland. His expedition was commissioned by Governor Palliser "to explore the unknown interior parts of Newfoundland; to examine into the practicability of travelling from shore to shore, across the body of that island; and to acquire a more certain knowledge of the settlements of the natives or Red Indians, as well as to surprise, if possible, one or more of these savages, for the purpose of effecting in time, a friendly intercourse with them." Cartwright's map of the river and of the east end of Lieutenant's Lake (now Red Indian Lake) is shown here. The drawing of the canoe is remarkably like the one drawn in the journal of the *Indeavour* in 1612.

In 1786 the youthful Prince William Henry, the future William IV, sailed to Newfoundland aboard H.M.S. *Pegasus*, performing on the coast the duties of a naval surrogate. The portrait is by Benjamin West. The log of the *Pegasus* on this voyage was richly illustrated by J. S. Meres and is one of the great sources for Newfoundland's pictorial history.

Entrance of St. John's Harbour

The entrance to St. John's harbour, from the logbook of H.M.S. *Pegasus*, 1786. The picture captures the British naval ascendancy over Newfoundland.

Views of Great St. Lawrence Harbour and Little St. Lawrence Harbour, from the logbook of H.M.S. *Pegasus*, 1786. British justice was being brought to the outharbours of Newfoundland.

A View of the upper part of Great St Lawrence Harbour

A view of Little St Lawrence Harbour

People

NEWFOUNDLAND IN THE EIGHTEENTH CENTURY was a harsh frontier of the British Empire, with a small and scattered population, primitive institutions in law and government, and few amenities of civilized life. Yet despite adverse conditions, the population along the shoreline of the Avalon peninsula was growing and, as the century progressed, spreading to the north and into the southern bays. There were approximately twelve thousand permanent residents in Newfoundland in 1700; around thirty thousand by 1790.

Gradually, the number of people of Irish origin came to equal the English. This early Irish population was formed from the countless thousands of servants transported annually to the fishing stations of Newfoundland from the port of Waterford and nearby harbours. Most of these migrant labourers returned to Ireland in the fall; but some stayed behind, settling in various outharbours of the Avalon and in St. John's, where eventually, with later immigrants, they grew into a numerically dominant political force. By the 1760s and 1770s they were already a volatile component in local society. Yet conditions in Newfoundland were so demanding that migrants from Europe had to adapt quickly. By 1765 it was possible for an observer to note that there were not only English and Irish in this nascent colony but also – evidently a separate breed – Newfoundlanders.

A view of the seven islands in the harbour of Placentia, from the logbook of H.M.S. *Pegasus*, 1786. The picture suggests that leisure and reflection were now also part of Newfoundland life. A civil society was emerging.

The beginnings of the Anglican church in Newfoundland date from the late seventeenth century (apparently there was a chapel in St. John's at the time of d'Iberville's raid of 1696), but it was not until 1784 that clergymen of other religions were officially permitted to minister to congregations on the island. However, Methodism in Newfoundland in fact dates from 1766, the year of Laurence Coughlan's arrival in Conception Bay, and a Congregational group began meeting in St. John's in 1775-76 under the leadership of a soldier, John Jones. And despite official proscription, Roman Catholic priests were known to be working among the people prior to 1784. In 1755, for example, it was discovered that a priest had said mass at Caplin Cove on the north shore of Conception Bay. He was tracked to Harbour Main by two justices of the peace, was fined £50, had his properties destroyed, and was ordered to leave the colony. He was found to be only one of two planter priests living in Harbour Main at the time. Meanwhile, in Labrador, the Moravians under Jens Haven were active among the Inuit from 1764, after an initial attempt in 1752 to make contact with them had failed.

The first schools on the island were opened under the auspices of the Society for the Propagation of the Gospel in Foreign Parts (SPG)—an Anglican missionary society dating from 1701, which did important work in fostering religion and education in Newfoundland and elsewhere. One such school was started in St. John's in 1744. At that date there was apparently a Roman

One of the significant events in the history of the Anglican Church in Newfoundland came during the visit of Prince William Henry, when he helped to found a "Protestant Chapel" in Placentia in 1786. In 1787 he gave its congregation this exquisite silver Communion service, comprising a flagon, a chalice, a paten, and an alms dish.

Catholic school in the capital as well. Coughlan, another SPG missionary (he was both an Anglican and a Methodist) kept a school open from 1767 to 1773 in Harbour Grace. The schoolmaster's salary was paid by the SPG. Other schools attached to SPG missions opened as the century drew to a close.

We know something about the life of the common people in smaller settlements from the accounts of the missionaries, especially those of the Methodists Coughlan and William Thoresby. We catch glimpses of a laborious, disaster-prone, tremulous existence, dominated by the elements. Yet towards the end of the eighteenth century a society in the making existed in Newfoundland. A zone of human occupancy had been carved out on the Avalon.

Extract from a document concerning the Inuit. The Danish missionary Larsen Christian Drachart came to Labrador in 1765, with Jens Haven and two other Moravian brethren, in order to found a mission in the region. In August, however, Drachart, who could speak Inuktitut but no English, found himself acting as interpreter for Governor Palliser, now seeking an economic *rapprochement* with the Inuit. On August 21, at Pitt's Harbour, Palliser struck a bargain with the Inuit. Part of the exchange that led to this arrangement is given here. It is in the form of a series of questions posed by Palliser, to each of which the Inuit answered yes. At the conclusion of the exchange, the Inuit accepted Drachart as "our teacher." Assisting in interpretation was the English Moravian, John Hill.

Study by Johann Valentin Haidt for his painting *Erstlingsbild* ("first fruits"). Executed in Herrnhut, the centre of the Moravian Church, in 1749, the study conveys the missionary zeal of the brethren. Note the Inuk, carrying a baby, below and to the left of the Christ.

Pen drawing of the Moravian establishment at Okak in northern Labrador in 1781. Part of the German inscription in the lower right corner has been translated as "Designed by Jens Haven." Haven was the founder of the Moravian Church in Labrador. The buildings are: 1. the church; 2. the lodging house; 3. the wash house, smithy, and bake house; and 4. the smoke house.

William Thoresby, who continued the work begun by Coughlan, preached on the circuit from Old Perlican, Trinity Bay, to Brigus, Conception Bay, from 1796 to 1798.

AN

ACCOUNT

OF THE

WORK OF GOD,

IN

Newfoundland, North-America,

In a Series of LETTERS,

To which are prefixed a few

CHOICE EXPERIENCES;

Some of which were taken from the Lips of Perſons,
who died triumphantly in the FAITH.

*O come hither, and hearken, all ye that fear God; and
I will tell you what he hath done for my Soul.*

To which are added, ſome excellent Sentiments,
extracted from the Writings of an eminent Divine.

Humbly Dedicated to the Right Honourable
The COUNTESS of HUNTINGDON,

By the Rev. L. COUGHLAN,

Late Miſſionary to the Society for propagating the
Goſpel in Foreign Parts, at *Harbour-Grace*, and
Carbonear, in *Conception Bay, Newfoundland*, and
now Miniſter of *Cumberland-Street Chapel*, London.

LONDON: Printed by W. GILBERT, No. 13,
Cree-Church-Lane, Leadenhall-Street; and Sold at
Cumberland-Street Chapel. 1776.

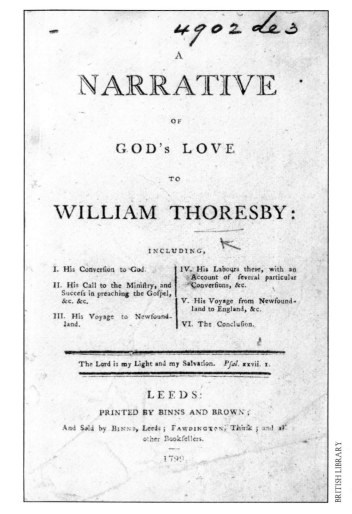

A

NARRATIVE

OF

GOD's LOVE

TO

WILLIAM THORESBY:

INCLUDING,

I. His Converſion to God.

II. His Call to the Miniſtry, and Succeſs in preaching the Goſpel, &c. &c.

III. His Voyage to Newfoundland.

IV. His Labours there, with an Account of ſeveral particular Converſions, &c.

V. His Voyage from Newfoundland to England, &c.

VI. The Concluſion.

The Lord is my Light and my Salvation. *Pſal.* xxvii. 1.

LEEDS:

PRINTED BY BINNS AND BROWN;
And Sold by BINNS, Leeds; FAWDINGTON, Thirſk; and at other Bookſellers.

1799.

Title page of Laurence Coughlan's account of his experiences as an Anglican priest and Methodist in Newfoundland. An Irishman who spoke the Irish language, Coughlan began his Newfoundland missionary work at Harbour Grace in 1766 and before his final departure from the colony in 1773 had established Methodist societies as far north as Blackhead in Conception Bay. In the winter of 1768-69 his followers at Blackhead constructed a church capable of holding four hundred people.

Title page of William Thoresby's account of his work in Newfoundland.

An eighteenth-century Roman Catholic chalice, the earliest extant in Newfoundland. It is dated 1768, and is Irish in origin.

John Jones, founder of the Congregational Church in Newfoundland. Born in Wales in 1737, Jones was serving in St. John's as a common soldier at the time of his conversion. This occurred when he heard a comrade, who had been mortally wounded in a brawl, blaspheme against the name of God.

The lawyer John Reeves arrived in Newfoundland in 1791 to preside over a new court of civil jurisdiction, which in 1792 became the supreme court of judicature of the colony. Reeves was also chief justice of this court. In 1793, having given evidence before a parliamentary inquiry on Newfoundland, he published his *History of the Government of the Island of Newfoundland*. His theme in this work was settler-West Country conflict, a topic that would pervade Newfoundland historiography.

The earliest known use in print of the word Newfoundlanders to describe residents of the island, as distinct from Irishmen and West Country men. It is in Griffith Williams's *An Account of the Island of Newfoundland* (London, 1765).

by Hundreds from *Ireland*: So that at the Time the *French* took the Country, the *Irish* were above six Times the Number of the West Country and *Newfoundlanders*: In short, they were in Possession of above three Quarters of the Fish Rooms and Harbours of the Island, who consequently received the French with open Arms. And during the

St. John's around the end of the
eighteenth century.

CHAPTER THREE

FISHOCRACY AND GOVERNMENT

The Making of Colonial Society

FROM 1775 TO 1815 the history of Europe, and to some extent North America, was dominated by war. The consequences in Newfoundland were profound. The American Revolutionary War had the effect of undermining the English migratory fishery, encouraging the production of local food supplies, and enhancing the status of St. John's as a port. When George Cartwright visited the town in 1786 he was "astonished" at the changes which had taken place since his visit sixteen years previously. Agriculture in the immediate neighbourhood was flourishing, the population had "greatly increased," "elegant houses" had been built, and merchants were living "comfortably, and even luxuriously." St. John's had been defended against privateers during the American war, while the outharbour trade and fishery remained dangerously exposed to attack by sea.

The Napoleonic Wars between 1796 and 1815 continued the process of eroding the transatlantic fishery, which could not function in wartime uncertainty. Inevitably, it was replaced by a fishery which was, as a governor noted in 1812, "decidedly sedentary." The population grew as the Newfoundland economy expanded, and a resident middle class of fish merchants, dealers, and professionals appeared in St. John's, whose stake was in the colony itself rather than in some remote county of England. This élite was Irish and Scottish as well as English. Soon they were demanding a say in government, and in the early nineteenth century a Society of Merchants was established in St. John's to promote the new entrepreneurial interests.

In 1808 the Scottish physician William Carson arrived from England, and within three years he was involved in political agitation, initially in collaboration with the merchants. The society he found in his new home was a curious anachronism in the history of the British colonies – mildly governed and loosely regulated, with a governor who came, as of old, for only a few months of the year. Yet the colony had year-round government of a sort. The kind of institutions that existed resembled those of eighteenth-century English counties, though a supreme court of judicature had been created in 1792. But at a lower level, magistrates, courts of quarter sessions, the grand jury, the sheriff, and constables helped to frame and uphold such regulations as existed, and thereby formed a kind of continuous local government throughout the year.

What Carson and the other reformers did was to try to replace old, local, informal, and to some extent voluntarist arrangements with partly elective government. Carson did not create government in Newfoundland; he substituted one form of government for another, and part of the resistance he met

was from an establishment which the old ways had created. Nor was the older system necessarily as harsh and rigid as the reformers later claimed. For example, title to land was still a confused and controversial question in the early nineteenth century, but in fact many residents had acquired extensive holdings in and near St. John's and acted as normal proprietors. (In the outports, as John Reeves said in 1793, "being removed from the Eye of Government, they make Inclosures, and carve for themselves almost as they please.") In any case, in 1813 the governor was empowered by the British authorities "to grant leases of small portions of land to industrious individuals for the purpose of cultivation." By 1831 Carson himself, despite alleged difficulties, had accumulated an estate of well over one

Christopher Spurrier came from a Dorset family long prominent in the Newfoundland trade. The sale announced here, the result of a bankruptcy, was an aspect of the decline of West Country influence in Newfoundland.

An announcement indicative of the burgeoning influence of the merchants in St. John's.

On Sale.

Valuable Mercantile
AND
Fishing Establishment.

FOR SALE, BY PRIVATE CONTRACT,

ALL those extensive, commodious, and excellent Premises, the property of CHRISTOPHER SPURRIER, Esq., situate at *Burin*, in Placentia Bay,

At a meeting of the Merchants' Society, held the 28th November last, at the Hall, the following Officers were chosen for the ensuing twelve Months.

JAMES MACBRAIRE, President.
STEPHEN KNIGHT,
JOHN DUNSCOMB,
NICHOLAS GILL, } Committee.
JAMES SIMMS,
THOMAS STABB, Treasurer.
JOHN GUEST, Secretary.

It having been reported to the Society of Merchants, that John Roche, John Keefe, James Keefe, and Michael Maher, used extraordinary exertions to save the lives of the unfortunate people in the Boat that was lost in the Narrows on the 4th instant;

The Society resolved, that a silver Medal should be given to John Roche, and he with the other three Men, should receive two Guineas each from the Funds of the Society.

A pound note issued on March 22, 1813, by the mercantile house of Shannahan's, whose premises in St. John's were bounded approximately by the present-day Long's Hill, Carter's Hill, and Duckworth Street. This firm also had premises at Ferryland. This is the first paper note issued anywhere known to feature the likeness of a woman. Such notes, private money, were in wide circulation in the colony at this time for commercial transactions of a small local nature. The earliest such note extant from Newfoundland was issued by Saunders, Sweetman, and Saunders at Placentia c. 1800.

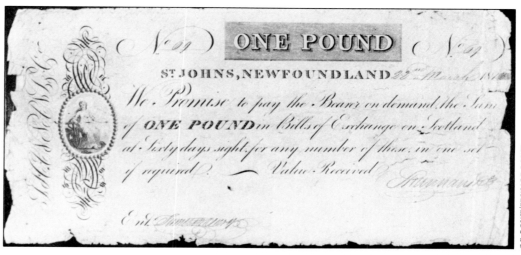

hundred acres.

Whatever its merits and defects, the old system slowly gave way, with Carson leading the assault. The collapse of the economy after the Napoleonic Wars created an atmosphere in which a reform movement could grow, though as early as November 1815 the governor was complaining that "a Party which affects a popular character" was on the increase in a "too easily agitated" St. John's. One reform came in 1817 when the colony was granted a year-round governor. In 1820 a surrogate court created a sensation by sentencing fishermen James Landergan and Philip Butler to whipping, and pressure mounted for judicial reforms. These were granted, with other important innovations, in a constitution in 1824.

In 1832 the colony was given representative government with elective and appointed chambers. Carson, though defeated in the first general election, entered the House of Assembly in 1833 through a by-election in St. John's. He had aligned himself with the insurgent Irish Catholics in St. John's and was openly supported in both elections by Bishop Michael Anthony Fleming.

Newfoundland now had the pleasures of electoral politics to savour. The taste proved bitter-sweet. After ten years of representative government, sectarian and political strife in the colony was so intense that the constitution of 1832 was suspended, and a new amalgamated legislature created, combining Upper and Lower Houses into one chamber. This novelty was in turn abandoned after five years, and the former consti-

---

This announcement illustrates the beginnings of professional life in St. John's in this period. Dawe, who was originally from Wales, became prominent in the reform movement in the colony in the 1820s, and was on occasion an emissary from the inhabitants to the imperial authorities in London.

W. DAWE, *Attorney & Solicitor*, respectfully informs the inhabitants of Newfoundland, that he has opened an Office on Church-hill, St. Johns.

Having been regularly bred to, and upwards of sixteen years in the profession in England, he trusts he is competent to conduct all business committed to his charge, to the satisfaction and interest of his clients.

☞ Letters from the Out-ports duly attended to.

Jan. 24, 1817.   12

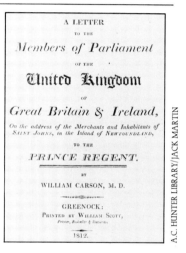

A LETTER
TO THE
Members of Parliament
OF THE
United Kingdom
OF
Great Britain & Ireland,
On the address of the Merchants and Inhabitants of SAINT JOHNS, in the Island of NEWFOUNDLAND,
TO THE
PRINCE REGENT.
BY
WILLIAM CARSON, M. D.
———
GREENOCK:
PRINTED BY WILLIAM SCOTT,
Printer, Bookseller & Stationer.
———
1812.

By this date, the ancient English institution of the quarter sessions of the peace was functioning well in Newfoundland. John Bland, an important local office-holder, was an opponent of the coming of representative institutions to the colony. He retired from the position of high sheriff in 1825 and died in 1826.

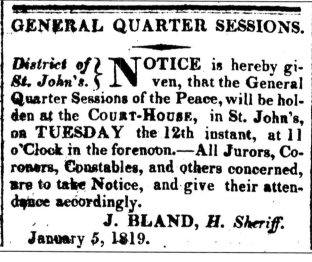

GENERAL QUARTER SESSIONS.

District of }
St. John's. } **N**OTICE is hereby given, that the General Quarter Sessions of the Peace, will be holden at the COURT-HOUSE, in St. John's, on TUESDAY the 12th instant, at 11 o'Clock in the forenoon.—All Jurors, Coroners, Constables, and others concerned, are to take Notice, and give their attendance accordingly.

J. BLAND, H. *Sheriff.*
January 5, 1819.

The first of William Carson's two political pamphlets, and the earliest literary expression of the need for political and judicial reform in the colony. He mentioned in this the "love of justice, and of liberty" which marked the residents of St. John's; he charged the governors with "ignorance" and denounced the naval surrogates for their lack of knowledge of "the most common principles of law." In a second pamphlet (1813) he said that if the governors continued to slight the people of Newfoundland, "admiration will be converted into contempt, affection to animosity, and submission to revolt." This incendiary last phrase expressed well his fiery spirit.

William Carson was born in Scotland in 1770 and entered the Faculty of Medicine at Edinburgh University. He came to Newfoundland in 1808, and three years later began agitation for constitutional reform. Carson mixed the practice of medicine with political, agricultural, and

literary pursuits. Philosophically a Whig, he was by nature suspicious of established authority and instinctively at odds with functionaries and governors who were seen to be exercising arbitrary power.

tution, with some slight alteration, restored. Reformers such as Carson, William Dawe, Patrick Morris, and John Kent had brought representative institutions to Newfoundland, but in bringing them had revealed deep and destructive cleavages within Newfoundland society.

The grand jury was yet another traditional English institution of justice and local government which had been brought to Newfoundland. In their presentments, the grand juries in various communities called the attention of public officials to pressing local needs.

ROYAL GAZETTE. 17 OCT. 1811

In July 1820 the surrogates Captain David Buchan (shown here) and the Rev. John Leigh found two Conception Bay fishermen guilty of contempt of court and sentenced them to be whipped. This gave Carson a great opportunity to advance the cause of reform in Newfoundland.

PANL/C1-213

Summary proceedings under Stat. 49th Geo 3 Chap. 27 —
Action of trespass — false imprisonment & tying *lif* to a flake and whipping him — Damages £1500 —
Special Jury impanelled and sworn —
Declaration 3 Counts &c
Plea General Issue under section 17 of Statute 49 Geo 3 and stating the Defendants acted as Surrogates —

PANL/GN5·2·A·1(1820-1)

The two fishermen, Butler and Landergan, were encouraged by Carson and others to take action against the surrogates in the Supreme Court. As shown here, Landergan's case was heard on November 9, 1820.

Chief Justice Francis Forbes was on the bench for the actions brought by Butler and Landergan. Although an opponent of the growing ambition of the reformers to achieve representative government, Forbes was known for his liberality and compassion. He found in favour of the two surrogates but in effect reprimanded them, and his judgment was by no means a defeat for the reformers. Forbes had been appointed chief justice in 1816 and resigned in 1822.

Part of Forbes's judgment in the Landergan case of 1820. The ultimate effect of the Butler and Landergan episode was to discredit the surrogate courts, which were replaced by a system of circuit courts in the new Newfoundland constitution of 1824.

— Holding this opinion still, the Court was bound to say that the Defendants were entitled to a verdict of acquittal — At the same time it must deprecate a mode of proceeding which disuse had rendered absolete in England, and which in every view of the present case, was particularly harsh and uncalled for — The Court could not but believe that the Defendants must have acted under some very gross misrepresentation of the facts of this case, or they had grievously mistaken the true object of the powers with which they were invested —

Sir Thomas Cochrane, governor of Newfoundland 1825-34. On his arrival in St. John's, he immediately swore in a council to assist him in administering the island. One of those sworn in, though he never voted or attended and was in effect subsequently disqualified, was Lieutenant-Colonel Burke, the officer commanding the military forces in the island at the time, and a Roman Catholic. Cochrane's approach to governing was constructive: he promoted the building of roads, reformed the system of poor relief, visited the outharbours, and generally attempted to conciliate the contending interests in the colony. His opposition to representative government was, however, well known in local circles, and before his departure from the island he had roused the antagonism of the reform party. The portrait is by R. Buckner.

Government House, by W.R. Best. Governor Cochrane planned the building of a residence in St. John's before leaving England. Construction began in 1827, and twenty-eight masons, twenty-five carpenters, and one slater were brought over from Scotland for the work. The building was completed in 1831 at a cost of £36,000, several times the original estimate. The ceilings of the main rooms were later decorated by a Pole named Alexander Pindikowsky. An art teacher, he did this work while serving a prison term given him in 1880 for forgery.

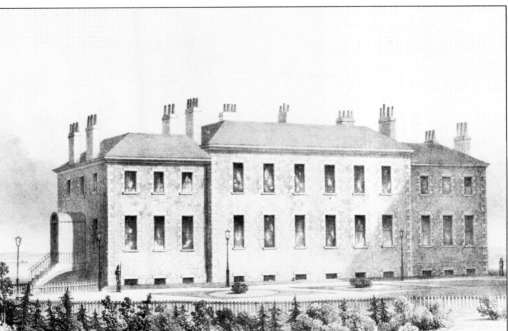

Patrick Morris, an Irish merchant, was drawn for the first time into reform politics by the Butler and Landergan incident. Born in 1789, he became in the 1820s a spokesman for Irish Catholics in St. John's and was one of Carson's most important allies. He took part in local agitation to have the Catholic Relief Bill of 1829 extended to Newfoundland, and he was later a member of the House of Assembly and colonial treasurer. He died in 1849.

PANL

Bishop Michael Anthony Fleming was born at Carrick-on-Suir, Co. Tipperary, Ireland, in 1792. A Franciscan, he arrived in Newfoundland in 1823. In 1829 he was consecrated Bishop of Carpasia *in partibus infidelium*, and on the death of Bishop Thomas Scallan in 1830 succeeded to the governance of the church in Newfoundland. Fleming was a zealous builder of Roman Catholic institutions and an outspoken supporter of the reform movement in the colony.

MERCY CONVENT/JACK MARTIN

The granting of a legislative assembly to Newfoundland in 1832 inspired this famous English cartoon, published as a broadsheet the same year by Thomas McLean in London. It is signed "HB" and was executed by John Doyle.

J.R. SMALLWOOD/R.D.W. PITT

ART GALLERY OF ONTARIO

Henry John Boulton, Chief Justice of Newfoundland, 1833-8. Boulton was given this appointment after a turbulent career in Upper Canadian politics. He and Henry Winton were the favourite objects of reform disdain in the 1830s. In October, 1837, the Queen was asked by the House of Assembly, now under the control of the reformers, to recall Boulton, and a delegation, including Carson, subsequently went to London to press this and other views.

Boulton went also. He was cleared of all charges of judicial impropriety, but the Judicial Committee of the Privy Council ruled that it was "inexpedient" for him to return to Newfoundland.

Henry Winton, journalist and publisher, was the owner and editor of the *Public Ledger* and an early supporter of the reform movement and Catholic emancipation in the island. In the early 1830s he savagely ridiculed a menacing mass movement of economic protest in Conception Bay, terming the insurgents in Harbour Grace and Carbonear a "lawless mob." After the election of the first general assembly late in 1832, Winton became a bitter and able enemy of the reform party and Bishop Fleming. On May 19, 1835, Winton was attacked on Saddle Hill while travelling on horseback from Carbonear to Harbour Grace. He was dreadfully beaten, his left ear cut off, and two pieces cut from his right ear. Despite the eventual offer of a reward of £1500, the perpetrators of the deed were never discovered. A proclamation offering an initial reward of £500 is shown here. The incident highlighted the drift of Newfoundland politics into sectarianism. A contemporary ballad ended with these lines: "Don't treat the poor Papists with scorn and with jeers/ Just remember what happened to Winton's two ears."

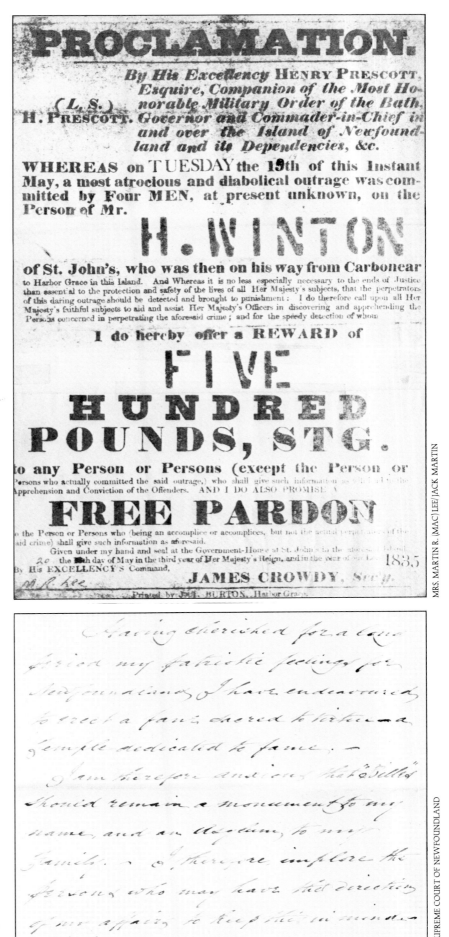

An excerpt from William Carson's last will and testament. He died on February 26, 1843.

Like many of William Carson's other enthusiasms, his plan for "Billies" also came to grief.

Sir John Harvey, Governor of Newfoundland, 1841-6. He presided over the introduction of the Amalgamated Legislature.

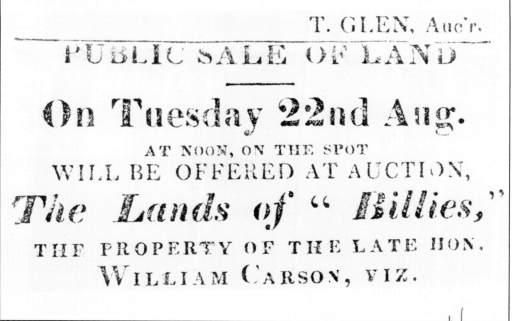

T. GLEN, Auc'r.

PUBLIC SALE OF LAND

On Tuesday 22nd Aug.

AT NOON, ON THE SPOT
WILL BE OFFERED AT AUCTION,

The Lands of " Billies,"

THE PROPERTY OF THE LATE HON.
WILLIAM CARSON, VIZ.

The Colonial Building in St. John's, the seat of the Newfoundland legislature, 1850-1934, 1949-59, a symbolic final meeting being held there by the Assembly in 1960. The cornerstone of the building was laid by Governor John Gaspard Le Marchant on May 24, 1847. The drawing is by W.R. Best.

Culture and Religion

As CONSTITUTIONAL CHANGE OCCURRED in the early nineteenth century, there was an intellectual and cultural awakening. John Ryan, a Loyalist from Rhode Island who had settled initially in New Brunswick, established Newfoundland's first printing press and first newspaper, the *Royal Gazette*, in 1807. Other papers quickly followed – the period 1810-50 was possibly the most vigorous in the history of Newfoundland journalism, with Henry Winton, John Valentine Nugent, and R.J. Parsons the leading luminaries in the field.

The intellectual life of the day can be measured by the fierceness of the newspaper rhetoric, and also by the number of associations and societies that were forming for a surprising variety of purposes. A "St. John's Library" existed as early as 1810, and the young naturalist Philip Henry Gosse discovered to his delight in 1827 that it was possible to glean "a sound knowledge of contemporary literature" from works available through the "Carbonear book club." Education was fostered through acts of the new legislature and by religious bodies, themselves expanding in influence. People were reading, arguing, building, hoping. Science, *belles-lettres*, and poetry were rearing their heads. And the scientific study of agriculture was beginning.

Meanwhile, national feeling was surfacing. In the 1840s the Newfoundland Natives' Society was formed, and for a while it was a potent force in local politics.

The logo of Newfoundland's first newspaper.

Established in 1815, this was Newfoundland's second newspaper.

The logo from the only known surviving copy of the third newspaper established in Newfoundland, and the first to espouse the cause of reform. It was founded in 1818.

The logo of Henry Winton's newspaper, established in 1820. On January 1, 1828, Winton changed the motto of the paper to: "Open to all parties – influenced by none." It was a sign of the times.

Drawing its membership exclusively from the native-born of European descent, it sought to rise above the ethnic and sectarian differences which had marked the previous decade and "to promote the general interests of Newfoundlanders." The society professed to have "nothing to do with religion" and to belong to "no party." But despite its idealism, the condition demanded for membership revealed further grounds for division within the colony. As the 1840s wore on, the influence of the society faded. The old differences which it had sought to overcome proved durable, and unity among the Newfoundland people remained elusive.

John Valentine Nugent, the leading intellectual and scribe among the Roman Catholic Irish in St. John's in the 1830s and 1840s. Nugent was born in Waterford in 1796, and arrived in St. John's in 1833. He wrote for the *Newfoundland Patriot*, and in 1841 became editor of the *Newfoundland Vindicator* which, though lasting less than two years, brilliantly expounded Catholic grievances. Driven under by libel suits, the *Vindicator* was resurrected as the *Newfoundland Indicator*. Nugent was also a controversial reform member of the House of Assembly. Henry Winton and John McCoubrey were fond of referring to him as John Vag. (for Vagabond) Nugent, but his qualities were undeniable. He died in 1874.

The opening of the Prospectus of the *Newfoundlander*, published May 17, 1827.

ON WEDNESDAY, FOURTH JULY NEXT,

WILL BE PUBLISHED,

THE FIRST NUMBER OF

"THE NEWFOUNDLANDER."

A WEEKLY NEWSPAPER.

PROSPECTUS.

AT the outset of an undertaking such as we are about to enter upon—namely, the Establishment of a Newspaper,—it is customary for the Proprietor to furnish those whose patronage he solicits, with a prospectus of some magnitude, containing promises and professions—the principles on which the paper is to be conducted, and even the very nature of the subjects to which its columns are to be devoted. It is hardly necessary to add—what must be known to every one—that such anticipations are generally found to have been made, at least in the majority of instances, with too much confidence, and without a very accurate calculation of the various difficulties which occur, to render it impossible, or impracticable, to carry them into effect.

THAT We, therefore, should not hereafter subject ourselves to the charge of inconsistency, or any deviation incompatible with the Rules which we have prescribed to ourselves in the conduct of the "NEWFOUNDLANDER": we shall at present briefly offer to the Public, the outline of our Plan, to which we beg leave to solicit their attention.

The logo of the *Newfoundlander*, a paper that was at once loyal and Irish.

This strongly conservative newspaper was founded in 1832 by John McCoubrey.

The *Patriot*, the organ of the reform party of Newfoundland, was founded in 1833 by William Carson. Henry Winton's derisory names for this paper were, among others, the *Pat-riot* and *The Lying Chronicle*.

The earliest Conception Bay newspaper.

In this period of general prosperity for Newfoundland, efforts of a voluntary and unofficial nature were made to bring relief to the poor. In 1793 John Reeves had noted that in Newfoundland it was "a common thing to give a Dollar to a Beggar."

St. John's was not all politics and fish in the early nineteenth century, as the advertisements in its many newspapers show. Horse-racing was an early and popular diversion.

Rowing contests were held in St. John's at least as early as 1818, and it is known that a regatta was held on Quidi Vidi Lake, the site of the race shown here, in 1829.

Such pleasures were by 1828 a regular feature of St. John's life. In May, 1820, the merchant Richard Morris told his sister in London that St. John's had no taxes or poor rates and that "the Poor have been Relieved this winter by an Amateur Theatre to which I am going tomorrow Evening with a Party of about a Dozen young Ladies to see the Opera of the Duenna." Harbour Grace had a "Play House" in 1824.

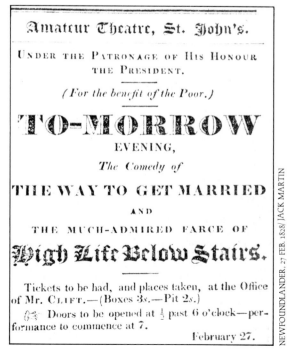

Mechanic's Society.

THE Members of the *St. John's Mechanics' Society*, purpose to dine together on TUESDAY, the 11th instant, to celebrate their first Anniversary.

☞ A list is now opened for signatures, at Mr. PATRICK DOYLE'S, *(Globe Tavern,)* which will be closed on Thursday, at 6 o'clock, p. m.

N. B.—*Dinner on the table at 6 o'clock.*

By order,
PATRICK KELLY,
Secretary.

March 5, 1828.

NEWFOUNDLANDER, 5 MAR. 1828/JACK MARTIN

AGRICULTURAL SOCIETY.

THE FIRST PLOUGHING MATCH.—This interesting exhibition took place on Wednesday last, and produced that calm species of excitement that never fails to be productive of considerable moral good. The ploughs entered were nine, but at an early period that of Mr. C. F. Bennett was obliged to be withdrawn, his very fine pair of horses being too spirited to afford a hope of success to the Ploughman.

The prizes were awarded by the Judges, in the following order :—

Mr. Reed's Plough,	1st prize.
Hon. Mr. Morris's	2nd do.
Mr. Coaker's	3rd do.

NFLD. PATRIOT, 29 JUNE 1842

Mechanics' Institutes were started in Great Britain in the early nineteenth century and were dedicated to the education of working men. The first such association in British North America was established in St. John's in 1827. Its founders had as their purpose the relief of "such of their Brethren as might from sickness or other casualties be rendered unable to work; also with the view to encourage and promote industrious habits, temperance, morality and obedience to the laws."

Agriculture was given greater prominence in Newfoundland life after the arrival of Sir John Harvey in 1841. The Agricultural Society which sponsored this ploughing match was formed the same year, with Carson as the first president and Harvey as patron.

A monthly *Farmer's Journal* appeared in St. John's in 1842.

The idea of a society to promote native interests originated in 1836 with the St. John's-born surgeon, Edward Kielley, who believed that "strangers had been sucking the vitals of the country." The first quarterly meeting of the Natives' Society was held on September 12, 1840, in John Ryan's fish store. The declaration shown here came in a speech made on this occasion by R.J. Parsons, editor of the *Newfoundland Patriot*. Another enduring Newfoundland cause had been born.

This night we proclaim ourselves a people—we proclaim our nationality, and we shall fail to do our duty, if henceforward we do not make that nationality to be respected.

PATRIOT, 15 SEPT. 1840

The Natives' Flag was next the subject of admiration. It was exhibited to the meeting beautifully sketched in pencil, and enclosed in a glazed frame. Mr. Richard Barnes explained the device. On either side of a shield appear two well-drawn figures, the one representing a fisherman or Sealer with the flag of the Society gracefully thrown across his arm—the other a Woodman with his dog, his rope and his axe. In the middle is a lovely group intended to represent the arts and sciences, &c. In one compartment of the shield is a codfish, in another a vessel in the Ice with her boat out returning with seals. In the opposite quarter is a Newfoundland Deer reposing under a fir tree ; and the other quarter exhibits a plough and a sheaf of corn. Over all are two clasped hands denoting unity, and above that a dove holding in her beak the olive branch of peace ; surrounding the whole is a wreath composed of the rose, thistle and shamrock, denoting the stock from whence the Newfoundlander derives his origin ; and underneath, forming a band for the motto " Union and Philanthropy," is a wreath of native strawberries. On the whole, forming as pleasing a picture as a Native would desire to see, full of meaning and intelligence. The society is indebted to the genius of a fair daughter of " Terra Nova " for the execution of this elegant device.

NFLD. PATRIOT, 15 SEPT. 1840

A description of a pencil sketch of the Natives' flag, exhibited at the meeting of September 12, 1840.

A version of the natives' flag, showing the clasped hands and, faintly, the word "Philanthropy."

THE OLD NATIVE FLAG

Monument in the churchyard of the Anglican Cathedral, St. John's, to Richard Barnes, a prominent figure in the Natives' Society. The first president of the society was Edward Kielley.

ERECTED
BY THE NEWFOUNDLAND
NATIVE'S SOCIETY
TO THE MEMORY OF
RICHARD BARNES
LATE OF ST. JOHN'S MERCHANT, N.H.A.
AND FOUNDER OF THE SOCIETY, WHO DIED SEP. 3RD 1846
THIS TRIBUTE IS A TESTIMONY OF HIS GREAT
TALENTS, MANY PRIVATE VIRTUES AND UNTIRING
EFFORTS FOR THE WELFARE AND ADVANCEMENT
OF HIS NATIVE COUNTRY.
1878.

In June, 1833, Bishop Fleming visited the Presentation Convent in Galway, Ireland, in order to recruit nuns to teach in Newfoundland. His purpose was to found on the island "a system of education, that... would smooth the pillow of sickness, and soften the rigours of winter, by the diffusion of true Christian feeling." The first volunteer to offer to go to St. John's was Sister Mary Magdalen O'Shaughnessy, shown here. She celebrated the Golden Jubilee of her arrival in Newfoundland in 1883, and died in 1889.

A party of four nuns left Ireland for Newfoundland on August 11, 1833, arriving in St. John's on September 21. Sister Mary Bernard Kirwan had been named Superior of the "intended convent." The nuns sailed to Newfoundland on the *Ariel*, whose master, shown here, was William Staunton. He died in St. John's in 1884.

The nuns brought their Irish curriculum with them to Newfoundland. Catherine Meaney's needlework is an early example of their success as teachers.

Programme
OF THE
ORDER of PROCESSION
IN MOVING
On THURSDAY, the 20th inst.
FOR THE PURPOSE OF LAYING THE
FOUNDATION STONE OF THE
New Cathedral.

At 12 o'clock, persons who are disposed to unite in this solemn ceremony will assemble in the vicinity of the Catholic Church, whence the procession will move by Queen-street, down the lower street, up the Beach, and by Cochrane street towards the Cathedral Ground in the following order:—

CROSS bearer
in Purple Tunic, and on each side of the Cross two Acolythes in white, carrying waxen torches.
The Band, three and three.
A Banner, with a painting of the present Pontiff Gregory XVI. borne by a person dressed in scarlet
A Carpenter carrying the Plans, supported on the right and left by two Masons, one bearing on a cushion a square and mallet, and the other on a similar cushion a square and trowel.
A Mason carrying on a cushion Plans of the Altars.
The Model of the Cathedral supported by four persons with sashes.
Masons two and two, with aprons.
Tradesmen in general, two and two.
A Painting of the Redeemer, carried by a person in white.
Female Children three and three.
Christian Doctrine Society, two and two.
Boys three and three.
A Painting of St. John, supported by two persons wearing white sashes on each shoulder.
Fishermen three and three.
Mechanics' Society, with their own banners.
Benevolent Irish Society, with their own banners, and preceded by two persons carrying the embroidered figure of St. Patrick.
Farmers three and three, preceded by one bearing a figure of Daniel O'Connell.
Gentlemen three and three.
A BAND.
A Banner, with a figure of the Queen.
Society of the Blessed Virgin Mary, three and three, preceded by two persons bearing a painting of the Blessed Virgin.
A Priest, carrying in his hands a copper box, containing the parchment with the inscriptions, coins, latest periodicals, &c. and supported on the right and left by two clergymen. one bearing in his hands a vase filled with Holy Water, and the other an Asperges.
Priests two and two.
Lastly—The Bishop supported by two Priests.

The laying of the corner-stone of the Cathedral of St. John the Baptist, from a contemporary commemorative medal.

The greatest nineteenth century building project of the Roman Catholic Church in Newfoundland was the Cathedral of St. John the Baptist in St. John's. The corner-stone was laid in May, 1841.

Roman Catholic Cathedral (now Basilica) of St. John the Baptist, St. John's. The first mass was said in the Cathedral in 1850, and the completed building was consecrated in 1855.

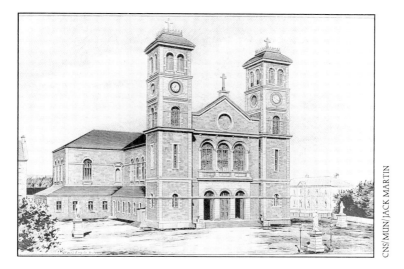

CNS/MUN/JACK MARTIN

The growth of Methodism in St. John's was another significant nineteenth century development, as the founding of a chapel in the capital in 1816 indicates. On June 7, 1798, a soldier, William Torrie, wrote that "there is no methodist Society at St. John's....We meet in the Garrison once a week in Class meeting by ourselves."

LINES
On laying the Foundation of the Methodist Missionary Chapel.

When Israel's sons with joyful shouts of praise
Began the Temple of their God to raise,
With tears of joy they wept in hopes to view
Their ancient structure equalled by the new.

To we who lately mourn'd our little fane,
With joy behold it rising once again;
Fondly anticipate it form'd complete,
And long impatient 'neath its roof to meet.

And should not *all* rejoice when any sect
A Temple to the Lord of Hosts erect,
If they glad tidings of salvation preach,
And in its purity the Gospel teach?

Religion, greatest comfort of mankind,
Should spread its precious blessings unconfined,
For what's that place religion does not bless,
A barren wild, a howling wilderness.

How should our hearts with gratitude expand
That God has given that blessing to our land;
O may he now display his saving grace,
And to his service consecrate this place.

Here may the saved their covenant renew,
And trembling sinners their salvation view,
And many a favour'd mortal, learn the road
That leads the faithful Christian to his God.

MERCANTILE JOURNAL, 21 SEPT. 1816

Methodist Church and parsonage in Carbonear, c. 1846. By this date Methodism had left its pioneer days behind in Conception Bay, and had become well established.

Aubrey George Spencer, first Bishop to the Anglican See of Newfoundland. Appointed in 1839, he was an energetic builder and organizer of his church in the new diocese. He laid the first stone of the Anglican Cathedral of St. John the Baptist in St. John's. This portrait of him was presented to the Cathedral by Miss F.J. Crowdy, Farnham, Surrey, England, in 1922.

Edward Feild, second bishop of the Anglican See of Newfoundland. He was born in Worcester, England, in 1801, and attended Rugby and Queen's College, Oxford. He was consecrated at Lambeth on April 28, 1844. In his church ship the Hawk he was a hardy traveller about the coasts of Newfoundland and Labrador. He died at Bermuda in 1876.

The nave of the Anglican Cathedral of St. John the Baptist in St. John's was consecrated on September 21, 1850. It was based on a design obtained by Bishop Feild from the celebrated English architect Sir George Gilbert Scott.

St. Bartholomew's Anglican Church, Harbour Breton, c. 1849.

The small but influential Scottish mercantile and professional community in St. John's was divided in the late 1840s between adherents of the Church of Scotland and those of the newly formed Free Presbyterian Church. The Free Church shown here, on Duckworth Street, St. John's, was opened in 1850. Immediately adjacent to it can be seen the St. John's branch of the Bank of British North America. The drawing is by W. R. Best.

BELOW
When the naval officer Edward Chappell visited St. John's in the summer of 1813, he noted the existence of "a public reading room" which displayed "English Daily Papers...and most of the British monthly Publications."

☞ NOTICE.

THE Subscribers to the ST. JOHN'S LIBRARY, are requested to send in the Books in their possession, by the 20th instant, that a more commodious and satisfactory plan may be arranged for issuing them at the General Meeting on the 1st of *December*—when each Subscriber is particularly desired to attend.
November 8, 1810.

Lewis Amadeus Anspach came to Newfoundland in 1799. An Anglican divine, he was appointed, in 1802, SPG missionary in Harbour Grace and Carbonear. He returned to England in 1812. His *History* has a rich social dimension, showing an intimate knowledge of local life.

William Eppes Cormack was born in St. John's in 1796, and was educated in the universities of Edinburgh and Glasgow. In 1822, in company with a Micmac Indian named Joseph Sylvester, he crossed the island on foot from Trinity Bay to St. George's Bay, the adventure taking about nine weeks. Cormack published a brief account of his adventure in 1824, and in 1856 his *Narrative of a Journey across the Island of Newfoundland* appeared as a book.

Samuel Codner, an English merchant in the Newfoundland trade, and founder in 1823 of the Newfoundland School Society. By 1826 the society had opened schools in St. John's and several other communities, and in time it ran as many as forty schools throughout the colony.

Philip Henry Gosse was born in Worcester, England, in 1818, and as a boy worked in the counting-house of the firm of George Garland and Sons at Poole. In 1827 he came to Newfoundland as a clerk in the Carbonear premises of Slade, Elson and Company. He left Newfoundland in 1835 for Compton, Lower Canada, where he farmed for three years. He then taught briefly in Alabama and returned to England in 1839. While in Newfoundland he made extensive studies of local insects, but a projected book, "Entomologia Terrae Novae" (1828-35), was never published. *The Canadian Naturalist* appeared in 1840 and *The Romance of Natural History*, containing a richly evocative account of "the opening of the day and the awakening of life" at Little Beaver Pond near Carbonear, in 1860. Gosse was a brilliant student of Newfoundland entomology and a shrewd observer of society in the Carbonear area. His son Edmund Gosse published *The Naturalist of the Sea-shore*, a biography of Philip Henry Gosse, in 1896. Gosse died in 1888.

William Charles St. John, by William Gosse, c. 1837. St. John, a close friend of Philip Henry Gosse, was born in Harbour Grace in 1806. In 1838 he was employed as a teacher, and in 1835 published A Catechism of the History of Newfoundland, an introduction to Newfoundland history written for children. Between 1845 and 1854 he edited the Conception Bay Weekly Herald, a newspaper of quality. In 1854, with his family, he emigrated to Boston, and died there in 1873.

John James Audubon. This world famous naturalist was born in Haiti in 1785. In 1833 he visited the North Shore of the Gulf of St. Lawrence, looking for specimens to include in his Birds of America (1827-38).

Another talented emigrant from Newfoundland was Philip Tocque (1814-99), who arrived in Boston in 1849. Tocque has been called the first Newfoundland-born man of letters. His books include Wandering Thoughts, or Solitary Hours (1846), Newfoundland: as it was, and as it is in 1877 (1878), and Kaleidoscope Echoes (1895). A Peep at Uncle Sam's Farm (1851) conveys his initial excited response to the attractions of the eastern United States. Of the thousands who moved to America from Newfoundland in the 1840s and 50s, many were tradesmen and professionals. Edward-Vincent Chafe, who has studied the

subject, has noted that "through emigration Newfoundland was being drained of its educated, its skilled, and its youth."

Audubon's drawing of the red-throated diver with the pitcher plant, the floral emblem of Newfoundland, in the background. On his return journey from the North Shore of the Gulf of St. Lawrence, Audubon stopped in at St. George's harbour, St. George's Bay, arrving on August 13, 1833. There he traded with Micmac Indians, exchanging pork and ship-biscuit for game. He also tasted bakeapples and paid "a quarter of a dollar" for a type of hare he had not seen before. On August 15 he recorded in his journal that he "spent a portion of the day in adding a plant to my drawing of the Red-necked Diver."

Black Swallowtail and Alexis Butterflies of Newfoundland.

A drawing from Philip Henry Gosse's "Entomologia Terrae Novae" (1828-35).

Robert Traill Spence Lowell, author of The New Priest in Conception Bay (1858), the first novel to be based on first-hand knowledge of Newfoundland life. He was an Anglican missionary in Bay Roberts from 1843 to 1847. An American, he was the brother of the poet James Russell Lowell, and himself wrote striking poems about Newfoundland.

Death of a People

ARCHAEOLOGICAL EXCAVATIONS conducted at a Beothuck house site in Boyd's Cove, Notre Dame Bay, in 1982 by Ralph Pastore uncovered about three hundred trade beads and four European pipe stems—evidence suggesting that some trading was carried on between the Indians and Europeans around the late seventeenth and early eighteenth centuries. By the middle of the eighteenth century the Beothucks apparently numbered about five hundred. By that date, according to Sir Joseph Banks, a trustworthy commentator, a "continual state of warfare" existed between them and the settlers. The English, he wrote,

"fire at the indians whenever they meet them, and if they chance to find their houses or wigwams, plunder them immediately." As settlement expanded around the island and European population grew, the Beothucks were driven back to a territory between the settlers in Notre Dame Bay and the hunting region of the Micmacs, to the south and west of Red Indian Lake. Their way of life, which depended on getting access to the seacoast, was doomed. As John Reeves noted in 1793, "instead of being traded with, they are plundered; instead of being taught, they are pursued with Outrage and with Murder."

In the early 1800s it was recognized that attempts had to be undertaken to save the people from extinction. Lieutenant David Buchan led an expedition to

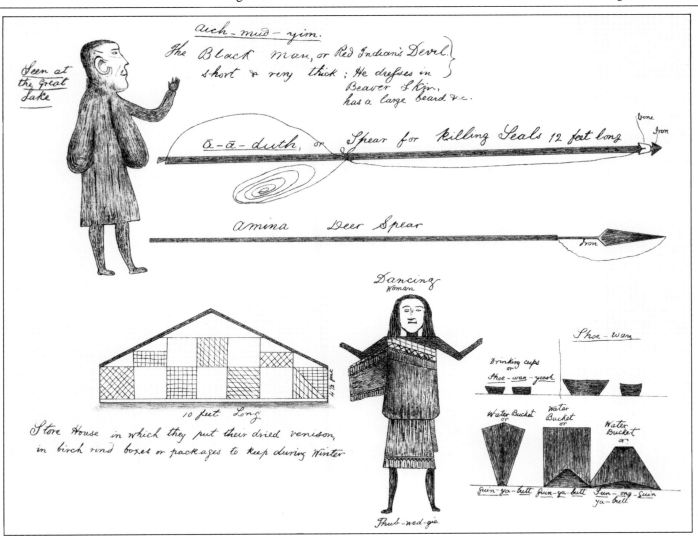

One of the ten drawings made
by Shanadithit while living in
St. John's.

Red Indian Lake in 1811 and found about seventy-five members of the tribe; but through bad luck and miscalculation this contact came to nothing. In March 1819, John Peyton Jr., who operated fishing premises in the Bay of Exploits, captured a Beothuck woman on Red Indian Lake in a bloody episode which saw her husband and possibly another Indian slaughtered. The woman was Demasduit (called also Waunathoake and, by the English, Mary March). She was conveyed to St. John's, where her portrait was drawn by the wife of Governor Charles Hamilton. The woman soon caught tuberculosis, and she died while Buchan was trying to return her to her people. At this point, early in 1820, it is reported that twenty-seven Indians remained alive.

Events were now rushing towards a grim finale.

William Cormack in 1822 undertook an exploratory walk across Newfoundland, one of his purposes being to locate Beothucks; he saw none. Less than a year later, in June 1823, a Beothuck woman and her two daughters were sent to St. John's after they had surrendered to a settler, William Cull. They were returned to Notre Dame Bay and spent some time in futile paddling along the coast, where it was hoped that they would meet other members of their tribe. While this sorry episode was in progress, the mother and one of the daughters, both suffering from tuberculosis, perished. The third, Shanadithit (called Nancy), who was aged between sixteen and twenty, proceeded to Exploits Burnt Island and became a servant in John Peyton's home. She remained in this obscure position for five

PANL/A17-105

John Peyton Jr., an Englishmen, came to Newfoundland c. 1812. He was a justice of the peace from 1818. Some have seen him as a menace to the Beothucks, but it has recently been argued that he was "a man of veracity and integrity."

Demasduit (or Mary March), by Lady Hamilton.

PAC/C87698

Shanadithit's skull and scalp were presented by William Carson, through the governor, to the Royal College of Physicians, London.

DIED, — On Saturday night, the 6th inst. at the Hospital, SHANANDITHIT, the female Indian, one of the Aborigines of this Island. — She died of consumption, a disease which seems to have been remarkably prevalent among her tribe, and which has unfortunately been fatal to all who have fallen into the hands of the settlers.

ROYAL GAZETTE, 16 JUNE 1829

years, acquiring some knowledge of English. She was then brought to St. John's and became a guest in the homes of William Cormack and Attorney General James Simms. In 1827 Cormack formed the Beothuck Institution and made another journey into the interior of the island in search of the tribe.

Shanadithit, last of the Beothucks, died in 1829.

This is an illustration from Charles A. Murray's *Ottawah, the Last Chief of the Red Indians of Newfoundland: a Romance* (London, 1847). Lost to history, the Beothucks had entered the realm of romance.

Town and Outport

As THE NEWFOUNDLAND FISHERY became island-based in character during and after the Napoleonic Wars, St. John's increased its economic hold over the outports, becoming, as a governor noted in 1814, "the Emporium of the Island." In the eighteenth century, Twillingate, Trinity, and Harbour Breton had frequent direct trading and supply links with England and other countries; but as the nineteenth century wore on, such commercial activity tended to be carried on through St. John's. One scholar has written that the nineteenth century outports became "increasingly introverted and isolated from the outside world." Nevertheless, until the second half of the century, Harbour Grace and neighbouring settlements maintained a vibrant economic life as centres of the seal and Labrador fisheries.

The hunting of seals from ocean-going vessels had begun in the 1790s, and by the 1830s had become a major contributor to the Newfoundland economy. Up to the 1850s, before the coming of steam, Conception Bay dominated the industry. The area also benefited greatly from the Labrador fishery, an annual migratory activity carried out from the northeast coast of the island but principally from Conception Bay. The Conception Bay "stationers" (or owners of Labrador fishing rooms) sometimes moved their entire families to the coast for the summer. Often, however, the fisherman went only with his crew, leaving his wife, children, and

A familiar early nineteenth century means of relieving distress and raising money for good causes.

NEWFOUNDLANDER, 5 MAR. 1828

A sketch of Carbonear, by Philip Henry Gosse, termed by him "A Cutting Out." It shows a passage being cut through the ice to allow sealing vessels to make their way to open water.

P.H. GOSSE, ZOOLOGY (1844)

relatives behind to tend gardens and look after farm animals. In addition to this stationer activity, there was also a "floater" fishery, consisting of schooners moving along the coast following the cod.

The Labrador fishery was a mainstay of Harbour Grace. From 1866 to 1870, the Labrador fleet from the town averaged eighty-one ships. The feats of navigation involved were remarkable. The fishermen moved stealthily from headland to headland, like the Greeks of old.

But it was the inshore cod fishery which remained the backbone of the Newfoundland outport economy. As the population expanded rapidly, more and more families in the outports grew dangerously dependent on the staple of cod and on a precarious subsist-

ence agriculture. It was a highly vulnerable economy, and throughout the nineteenth century, as the fish and potato crop from time to time failed, people experienced great distress - compelling governments to step in with whatever welfare assistance they could muster, usually not much, and grudgingly given. The relationship which developed between the fishermen and the government was one of dependency, as was that between the fishermen and the merchants, with the merchants extending credit in the hopes of a good and profitable catch. It was a barter, or "truck", system in which the merchant, controlling prices, had the upper hand.

Newfoundland outport society was shaped in the nineteenth century as horizons narrowed, dependency

This anonymous 1832 notice of a meeting near Carbonear shows the division that had arisen in Newfoundland by the time of Representative Government between merchants and fishermen. The meeting in question was attended by about two thousand men. Rechristening Saddle Hill "Liberty Hill," they passed resolutions calling for the abolition of the truck system.

PANL/GN2/2 (JAN.-MAR. 1832)

grew, and the struggle to ward off impoverishment dominated life. The making of a living was a familial process, with all hands adding their labours to take advantage of seasonal opportunity. However, there were periods of prosperity in some outports. And if one aspect of these communities was sometimes poverty, another was a small-propertied self-reliance.

In the meantime, the capital was developing its own unique hierarchy and experiencing its own successes and sufferings. Fire was a particular threat in St. John's and Harbour Grace. But this was not the only source of anxiety. The operations of the big merchants in St. John's were huddled together on the south side of Water Street, while on the hill behind were densely packed labourers, many of them Irish and renters – a menacing political presence.

A first-generation cottage, near Trinity, c. 1850.

DAVID B. MILLS

Greenspond, Bonavista Bay, in
1846, by Rev. B. Smith.

Grand Bank, c. 1849

Scene on the north-west arm of
Trinity, c. 1849.

The town and harbour of St.
John's, taken from Signal Hill,
June 1, 1831, by William Eager.

The growth of St. John's in the early decades of the nineteenth century was constantly imperilled by the threat of fire. In the long run, attempts at fire protection such as the one illustrated here did not succeed. A major conflagration occurred on February 12, 1816, and smaller but still very damaging fires on November 7 and 21, 1817. In the great fire of June 9, 1846, the work of a generation was largely undone.

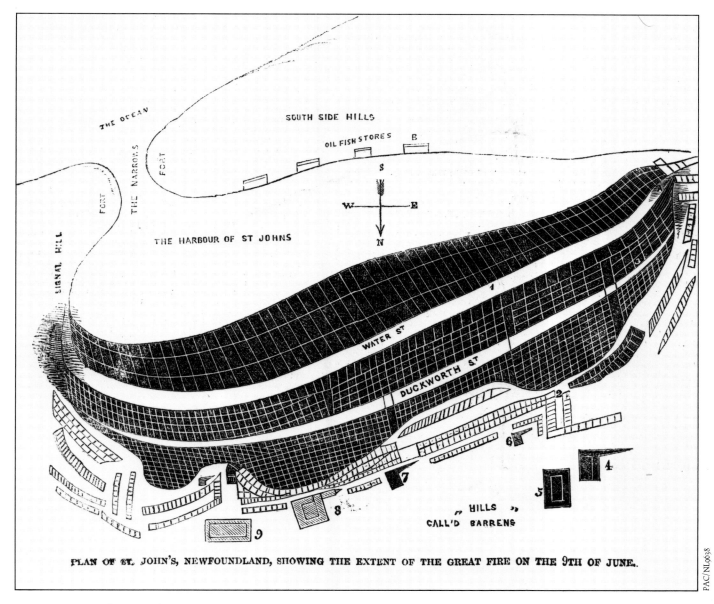

PLAN OF ST. JOHN'S, NEWFOUNDLAND, SHOWING THE EXTENT OF THE GREAT FIRE ON THE 9TH OF JUNE.

PAC/NL9038

A contemporary sketch of the damage caused by the fire of 1846, from the *Illustrated London News* (July 4, 1846).

Schooners at Indian Harbour, Labrador.

CHAPTER FOUR

"The Drama of the Sled and Dory"

Responsible Government

NEWFOUNDLAND MOVED from representative to responsible government roughly in step with the other British North American colonies, the change occurring in 1855. But local circumstance as well as imperial policy shaped the new system. Sectarianism was especially notable both before and after the event.

The leading advocates of constitutional reform in Newfoundland in the early 1850s were the Roman Catholics Philip Francis Little and John Kent and the Protestant R. J. Parsons. Behind their Liberal party stood John Thomas Mullock, who had become Bishop of St. John's in 1850. The first premier under responsible government was Little and the first colonial secretary Kent. In the election of 1855 the Liberals carried eighteen of thirty seats. Fifteen of the eighteen Liberal members were Roman Catholics, but Little tried to overcome this imbalance by including two Protestants in his cabinet. The leader of the opposition in the first assembly under responsible government was Hugh Hoyles.

In 1858, Little was succeeded as premier by Kent, who won an election the following year. His victory was, however, marred by sectarian violence at Harbour Grace and by charges from Hoyles and Edward Evans, who were defeated in Burin, of Liberal electoral improprieties. Then, in 1860, Bishop Mullock turned on the Kent government for failing to provide an outport steamer service. Shortly after this, there was an uproar within the government party over the method of distributing poor relief. The climax to Kent's troubles came in 1861 when he charged in the House that the withdrawal of a government-sponsored currency bill had been forced by a combination of the governor, Sir Alexander Bannerman, the Opposition, and certain judges who objected to being paid in Newfoundland, rather than British, funds.

When Kent refused Bannerman's request that he verify his charges as reported in the press, Bannerman dismissed him from office, whereupon Hoyles became premier. A riotous election followed with Protestant-Catholic clashes occurring in St. John's, Harbour Grace, and Carbonear. In Harbour Main district internecine Catholic strife led to an incident in which one man was killed and nine others injured.

Hoyles carried the 1861 election by fourteen members to twelve, but Harbour Main and Harbour Grace districts (each entitled to elect two members) were not represented in the new House, ostensibly because of election irregularities. Nevertheless, the two men who had led the polls in Harbour Main – G.J. Hogsett and Charles Furey – attempted to take seats when the House of Assembly met on May 13. Their removal from the Assembly touched off fierce rioting

in St. John's in which three people were fatally injured. Only the timely intervention of Bishop Mullock restored an uneasy calm.

These events did not augur well for the future of either responsible government or religious toleration in Newfoundland. But in fact sectarianism would never again be such a powerful force in local politics. Hoyles's hold on power was strengthened by victory at the polls in Harbour Grace in November 1861, and an elaborate denominational truce, based on the judicious distribution of patronage at every level, was gradually worked out in Newfoundland. This survived well into the twentieth century, when it was finally eroded and made irrelevant by the grinding equalizers of secularism, consumerism, bureaucracy, and the like. Nine-

Philip Francis Little, first premier under responsible government. Born in Prince Edward Island in 1824, he began the practice of law in St. John's in 1844. In 1858 he became Puisne Judge of the Supreme Court of Newfoundland. He died in Ireland in 1897.

Bishop John Thomas Mullock. He was born in Limerick, Ireland, in 1807 and arrived in St. John's in 1848. His criticism of the established order in Newfoundland and his support for responsible government were open and direct. In 1852 he wrote to Little: "Acquainted as I am with many forms of government, having lived and travelled in many lands, having paid some little attention to the history of despotic and constitutional governments, I solemnly declare that I never knew any settled government so bad, so weak, or so vile as that of our unfortunate country; irresponsible, drivelling

despotism, wearing the mask of representative institutions, and depending for support alone on bigotry and bribery." The letter found its way into the local press.

John Kent, the second premier under responsible government, was born in Waterford, Ireland, in 1805. In 1859 Kent, as premier, was appointed to an Anglo-French commission of inquiry into fishery problems around the coasts of Newfoundland. It was the pinnacle of his career. He is shown here embarking for London and his diplomatic work, on board the Galway steamer *Pacific*.

CNS/COAKER PAPERS/JACK MARTIN

PRESENTATION CONVENT/JACK MARTIN

ILLUSTRATED LONDON NEWS, 30 APR. 1859

teenth century Newfoundland has been called "John Bull's other Ireland"; but in the long run, Newfoundland's history would afford a notable contrast to Ireland's continuing communal strife.

Sir Hugh Hoyles, premier from 1861 to 1865, and chief justice, 1865-80. He was born in St. John's in 1815, and was the first native Newfoundlander to hold the office of premier.

Sir Alexander Bannerman, Governor of Newfoundland from 1857 to 1864.

I as the leader of the late Executive, feel deeply wronged. For the severe discharge of my duty I have been sacrificed. I have fallen, not by the action of the Constitution; I have been victimised by an intrigue. The seat of this intrigue was Government House — the Chief actor — Governor Bannerman.

John Kent's comment on Governor Bannerman to the Duke of Newcastle, British Colonial Secretary, June 5, 1861.

✝ JOHN THOMAS,

By the Grace of God, and favour of the Apostolic See, Bishop of St. John's.

TO THE FAITHFUL OF THE DIOCESE OF ST. JOHN'S, HEALTH AND BENEDICTION IN THE LORD.

DEARLY BELOVED,—

As you have now returned from the dangers of the Fishery, and we are about to enter on the Holy Season of Advent to prepare for the great Feast of the Nativity of our Lord, when the Angels proclaimed "Peace on earth to men of good will," we gladly take this opportunity of addressing you, hoping you will listen to the voice of your Pastor, whose only anxiety is for your spiritual and temporal welfare. The last blessing our Saviour gave to his Disciples was that announced at his birth place, "My peace I leave you, my peace I give you." This greatest of all blessings has been too often disregarded, and it is to call your attention to it that we now address you. By violating the laws, by breaches of the peace, you not only injure your own souls—for no man should resist the higher powers—but you ruin yourselves and your families, and you only do the work of your enemies. The man who commits an outrage against person or property is the greatest enemy of his faith and of the principles it inculcates: while he is pining in a prison and his family in want he not only suffers himself, but his punishment is made a cause of reproach to his Church. Think not, dearly beloved, that we and our Clergy do not deeply feel ▬▬▬ ▬▬▬ and sympathise with your misfortunes. We may truly say with St. Paul "Who is weak and I am not weak? who is scandalised and I am not on fire?" Cor. 11. 29. It is on this account that we earnestly implore you to avoid all quarrels, to shun all riotous proceedings. The holy season of Advent will open with the Devotion of the forty hours Adoration. The Most Holy Sacrament will be exposed to the adoration of the faithful for three days. Every evening there will be a Solemn Benediction; and a Procession of the Most Holy on Tuesday, the last evening, at 7 o'clock. Attend assiduously as far as your avocations allow you at this Devotion. Shun drunkenness, the root of all evil in this Country. The drunkard, as sometimes seen in our streets, no matter to what class he may belong, is a disgrace to human nature itself.— We call on parents to use every endeavour to oblige their children to return to their homes at an early hour: the practice of youths by haunting corners and sometimes annoying the passers-by cannot be too strongly reprobated; it has led to a great deal of mischief, it may lead to worse. Prepare yourself, especially you who have been all the summer engaged in the Labrador or Outharbor Fishery, to receive worthily the Sacraments of Penance and the Holy Eucharist, your Christmas duty. Let us all devoutly pray that God may infuse into our souls the spirit of charity, that on the approaching great Festival we may be able with pure lips and hearts to join in the hymn of Angels "Glory to God on High and peace to men of good will."

The grace of Our Lord Jesus Christ be with you.

✝JOHN THOMAS.

ST. JOHN'S,
Feast of All Saints.

Rev. Charles Pedley, author of *The History of Newfoundland from the Earliest Times to the Year 1860* (1863). He was the minister of the Congregational Church in St. John's. Given the tenor of his times, it is not surprising that Pedley, in his *History*, singled out "religious distinctions" as one of his themes.

Bishop Mullock's pronouncement, towards the end of the turbulent year 1861.

Confederation

NEWFOUNDLAND WAS NOT REPRESENTED at the Charlottetown Conference in September 1864, the formal beginning of the events leading to Confederation, but the Hoyles government sent two delegates to the Quebec Conference the following month. They were Ambrose Shea, the Roman Catholic leader of the Liberal opposition, and Frederick B. T. Carter, the Speaker of the House of Assembly. But the farthest the Newfoundland House of Assembly was willing to go after the Quebec Conference was to pass a resolution in March 1865, which stated that, "having regard to the comparative novelty and very great importance of this project, it is desirable that before a vote of the Legislature be taken upon it, it should be submitted to the consideration of the people at large."

The next month, Carter became premier of Newfoundland, forming a coalition government which included Shea. This dramatic development was followed by a general election in November; Carter's government was sustained in this contest, but his followers could by no means be described as constituting a confederate party. Although Confederation had been an issue in the election campaign, the Carter government had clearly not been given a mandate to accept the Quebec resolutions and it did not do so. One St. John's newspaper reported after the election that of sixteen anti-confederates in the assembly, eight

Part of the Confederate case in 1869.

REASONS WHY

THE PEOPLE OF THIS COLONY SHOULD WISH TO BECOME CONNECTED WITH THEIR FELLOW-COLONISTS OF CANADA, NOVA SCOTIA AND NEW BRUNSWICK.

1st.—Because the condition of this country for some years past, proves the necessity of some important remedial change in our affairs.

2nd.—Because if such change be not effected, a large number of the people must leave the country for want of means to live in it.

3rd.—Because capital is being withdrawn from the trade, and there is no chance of maintaining even the present means of employment if we continue to rely on existing resources.

4th.—Because the population are broken down by poverty, and there is no hope in the future for the rising generation unless we can improve our condition.

5th.—Because it is found that wherever a Union of countries takes place on just and honourable conditions, the Union is strength, and leads to prosperity, as in the case of the United States of America.

6th—Because the proposed Union with the neighbouring provinces will be on the terms of fair and equitable partnership (which terms will be guaranteed by the Imperial Government), in which equal rights will be secured and the interest of all will be to uphold one another and protect the common welfare and prosperity.

NEWFOUNDLANDER. 10 SEPT. 1869

were government supporters. Given this political situation, Carter's reluctance to press forward with the Quebec resolutions is easy to understand.

During the 1866 session of the assembly Confederation was discussed in Committee of the Whole but the members decided that it was not "expedient" to debate it "with a view to any decision thereon." In keeping with the imperial government's support for Confederation, Governor Anthony Musgrave did everything he could to advance the cause of union but made little headway. In the circumstances the London Conference of December 1866 was only of passing interest in Newfoundland. Nor did the realization of Confederation on July 1, 1867, make much difference in the colony. By 1868 it was clear that confederates and anti-confederates were almost evenly balanced in the Newfoundland House and that the negotiation of terms of union with Canada would be impossible.

The next year, however, confederate prospects seemed to brighten considerably. Locally, factionalism developed among the anti-confederates, while in Canada Prime Minister Sir John A. Macdonald completed the brilliant set of political manoeuvres by which he pacified Nova Scotia. These events emboldened Newfoundland's confederates, and Governor Musgrave in his speech from the throne on January 28 opening a new session of the legislature said that public opinion was "ripe" for dealing with Confederation. Subsequently, resolutions embodying a scheme of union were approved by the legislature and a delega-

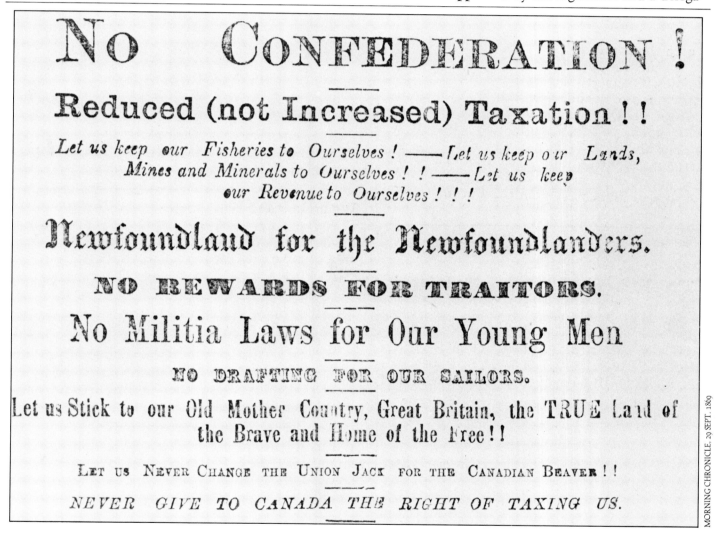

NO CONFEDERATION !

Reduced (not Increased) Taxation ! !

Let us keep our Fisheries to Ourselves ! —— Let us keep our Lands, Mines and Minerals to Ourselves ! ! —— Let us keep our Revenue to Ourselves ! ! !

Newfoundland for the Newfoundlanders.

NO REWARDS FOR TRAITORS.

No Militia Laws for Our Young Men

NO DRAFTING FOR OUR SAILORS.

Let us Stick to our Old Mother Country, Great Britain, the TRUE Land of the Brave and Home of the Free ! !

LET US NEVER CHANGE THE UNION JACK FOR THE CANADIAN BEAVER ! !

NEVER GIVE TO CANADA THE RIGHT OF TAXING US.

MORNING CHRONICLE. 29 SEPT. 1869

Anti-Confederate propaganda
from 1869.

tion despatched to Ottawa. When success was achieved there also, Carter sought the approval of the electorate for his grand design. His leading anti-confederate opponent in the bitterly fought campaign which followed was Charles Fox Bennett, a St. John's businessman who had opposed the introduction of responsible government.

Carter's cause met with diverse and widespread opposition. It was especially unpopular among the Roman Catholics, Shea notwithstanding. But emotionalism aside, there was no real economic basis for the union of Newfoundland with Canada in the 1860s. Newfoundland had a paltry export trade with British North America, and while her import trade with the region was more important, her major suppliers were elsewhere, the largest being the United Kingdom.

Mercantile opinion was divided on the issue of Confederation, and the result of the 1869 election was no surprise: twenty-one of the thirty members returned were opposed to Union with Canada. The constituencies which returned confederate members were Harbour Grace (two members), Bay de Verde, Carbonear, Trinity Bay (two members out of three), Burin (two members) and Burgeo and LaPoile. Their successor constituencies, with the exception of Harbour Grace, would vote for Confederation again in 1948. After the election Bennett was called upon by a new governor, Sir Stephen Hill, to form a government, and he remained in office until 1874.

Sir Frederick B.T. Carter. He was born in St. John's in 1819. A lawyer, he was premier, 1865-70, 1874-8, and chief justice, 1880-1900.

PANL/B1-151

PAC/C54438

Charles Fox Bennett. Though an old man in 1869, he led a vigorous campaign against Confederation. Bennett was an early promoter of mineral development on the island.

PANL/B1-145

Sir Ambrose Shea. He was born in St. John's, and was a businessman and member of the House of Assembly, 1848-69, 1874-87. He became governor of the Bahamas in 1887.

PAC/C64318

Sir Stephen Hill, governor of Newfoundland, 1869-76. On November 20, 1869, Hill wrote as follows to Earl Granville, the British Colonial Secretary: "The Mass of voters in this Colony as already stated by me in a former Despatch are an ignorant lawless, prejudiced body, the majority of whom living as they do in the Outports in almost a primitive state of existence are unfit subjects for Educated and Intellectual men to attempt to reason with on the advantages of Confederation. I therefore consider that it was a fatal error to have submitted to such a population the decision of such an important question as the Union of this Country with Canada."

The French Shore

THE TREATY RIGHTS which France had been given on Newfoundland's shores and in the adjoining territorial waters became a source of great resentment in the colony during the nineteenth century, especially in mercantile St. John's. Much of this ire was directed at the imperial authorities, who for long denied the government in St. John's full sovereignty over the island, in the name of upholding international agreements.

Yet there was less than unanimity in Newfoundland itself on the issue, despite the bombast heard in the capital. On the south coast of the island a lively, if illicit, trade was carried on for much of the century with the French islands of St. Pierre and Miquelon (which grew in population from about five hundred in 1820 to approximately five thousand in 1870). St. John's businessmen considered that Newfoundlanders who sold bait to the French were feeding the industry of one of the colony's important fish-marketing rivals, but they were never able to stop such practices.

A similar indifference to St. John's and its quest for sovereignty seems to have existed on parts of the French Shore also. The population of this long coastline was only 3,334 in 1857, but it grew to 17,234 by 1901. In relative terms this represented a change from 2.7 per cent to 7.9 per cent of Newfoundland's population. Government was remote from this scattered and for

Henry Labouchere, first Baron Taunton, by Bertel Thorvaldsen. He was born in 1798 and educated at Winchester and Christ Church, Oxford. He was secretary of state for the colonies at the time of the Anglo-French agreement of 1857. His despatch to Governor Charles Darling of Newfoundland on March 26, 1857, withdrawing this agreement, was hailed by many Newfoundland public figures as a kind of local Magna Carta.

The key passage in Labouchere's despatch of 1857.

The proposals contained in the Convention having been now unequivocally refused by the Colony, they will, of course, fall to the ground. And you are authorized to give such assurance as you may think proper that the consent of the Community of Newfoundland is regarded by Her Majesty's Government as the essential preliminary to any modification of their territorial or maritime rights.

I have the honour to be,
Sir,
Your obedient servant,

long unenfranchised population. Visited annually by ships of the Royal Navy, the French Shore was the island's frontier – at once promising but disputed.

In January 1857 Great Britain, in the face of mounting difficulties, negotiated a new agreement with France which would have significantly altered the terms of the eighteenth-century arrangements. Britain had never admitted France's claim to exclusive fishing rights off the French Shore but now proposed to accept this, as well as the exclusive right of French fishermen to use the shore for related activities in certain areas, namely from Cape St. John to Cape Norman, and at Port au Choix, Small Harbour, Port au Port, Red Island, and Codroy Island.

Newfoundland took strong exception to these arrangements – the din of opposition uniting Liberal and Tory, Catholic and Protestant. Britain conceded this round to colonial opinion, but the French Shore question in its many aspects would complicate relations between St. John's and Whitehall for almost another half century.

In the 1860s Newfoundland sought imperial sanction for the making of land grants on the French Shore and the appointment of resident magistrates, though the latter reform met with some local resistance. In 1869 London gave limited approval for the establishment of normal property rights in the area and in 1877 agreed to have a magistrate on the coast, provided he was

Wigwam of the *Micmac Indians*, in *St. George's Bay, Newfoundland.*

E. CHAPPELL, VOYAGE (1818)

Micmac Indian wigwam at St. George's Bay on the French Shore, c. 1813. According to Ralph Pastore, the earliest written account of Micmac contact with Newfoundland is dated 1602. This historian has also described the nineteenth century as "a kind of Indian summer" for the Newfoundland Micmacs, "an interval of relatively little interference from whites and a time when they could live much as their ancestors had." No doubt as far as the west coast was concerned, the French Shore question, by limiting Newfoundland sovereignty, contributed to the freedom they enjoyed. The Micmacs were great hunters and trappers and knew the interior of the island well. As Cormack's exploration had shown, they would guide the white man into this region. In the 1820s the Micmacs in St. George's Bay were using a schooner of their own construction as well as their traditional modes of transport.

answerable to the imperial government on any point affecting the agreements with France. Newfoundland thus made gains, but the territorial hegemony she desired remained elusive. The wonder is that her loyalty to Queen and Empire withstood so severe a test of her territorial integrity.

View of Conche on the French Shore. This French photograph, along with those of L'Ile Saint-Jean and Sandy Point, were "handed by the French Commissioners to their Colleagues" at the twentieth meeting of the International Commission for Newfoundland Fisheries, held in St. John's on board H.M.S. *Gassendi*, August 16, 1859. Members of the Commission were: Hugh Dunlop, John Kent, Marquis de Montaignac, and Cte. A. de Gobineau.

PRO/CO 194/160/f.171

PRO/CO 194/160/f.170

View of the harbour of St. John Island on the French Shore, c. 1859.

95

Sandy Point, St. George's Bay,
part of the nineteenth century
French Shore, c. 1859.

Daniel Woodley Prowse. Born
at Port de Grave, Conception
Bay, in 1834, author of the
magisterial A History of
Newfoundland from the English,
Colonial, and Foreign Records (1895).
Interested in every aspect of
what he called "this queer
country," Judge Prowse had a
special mastery of
Newfoundland's international
entanglements. "The way," he
wrote in 1902, "in which we fall
down and worship the alien
tramps that drift to our shores
is most comical."

Judge Prowse's comments on
the people of St.George's Bay,
in a letter to the colonial
secretary of Newfoundland,
G.D. Shea, May 29, 1879.

Sir.

During my late visit to St Georges
Bay I deemed it my duty to make
myself thoroughly acquainted with the
feelings of the people and their wants
and wishes — They have been a very
long time without paying duties, they
are therefore naturally disposed to
the "ignorant impatience of taxation"
which is not unknown. Elsewhere —

Return of Corner Brook
School, Bay of Islands N.F.L.

For the year beginning Dec 11th 1876, ending Dec 7th 1877
No. of days school was open 244.

Name of Teacher — Miss Margaret Tupper
No. of boys — 19
"   girls — 30
Total — 49
" between 5 & 15 years of age — 46
"   "   "   " not attending but near, about 20 who cant read or write
Fees charged — 50¢ per month
Total amount of fees — $141.00
"   "   " paid — 105.00
Salary promised — 160.00 & board
"   paid — 145.00 . ($40.00 from private parties)
Public Examination. 1. Ap 3   2. Dec 7
No visitors to school during year. 48.
Basis on which Established. Protestant, but unsectarian
    Fees to all on the same terms, No religious test
    All denominations attend.

No other school accommodation provided for these children
The Teacher has been engaged for another half year.

We do certify that the statements contained in this return, so far
as we know are correct in every particular

John Tupper   Trustees
Charles P Farnell   appointed by those
                      establishing the
                      School.

Margaret Tupper.   Teacher

Annual report of the school at
Corner Brook on the French
Shore, 1877.

Fish and Railway Politics

As NEWFOUNDLAND'S QUEST for economic development grew more complex and determined after 1869, so too did her international entanglements, which were now with the United States as well as Britain and France. In 1854 Britain had been able to obtain from the United States important trading concessions for the British North American colonies, in return for special rights for American fishermen along their Atlantic coastline. This agreement laid to rest for the moment a long-standing dispute over the meaning of the fisheries provisions of the Anglo-American Convention of 1818. But the abrogation of the Reciprocity Treaty by the United States in 1866 stirred that issue once more.

A further negotiation followed in 1870 in the aftermath of the American Civil War. On this occasion, John A. Macdonald was one of the British commissioners, but Newfoundland was not given a direct voice in the talks. The bargain that was now struck – in the Treaty of Washington of 1871 – was most unsatisfactory to Canada and was only grudgingly accepted by the dominion government. In effect, it renewed the fishing privileges Americans had enjoyed after 1854 but gave Canadians much less than had been obtained in that year.

One feature of the settlement, however, ultimately displeased the United States. This called for cash compensation to Britain if her claim could be substantiated that she had given more in certain of the fishery articles

Sir William Whiteway, Newfoundland's late nineteenth century "Apostle of Progress." He was born in Devon in 1828, and was premier of Newfoundland, 1878-85, 1889-94, 1895-7. His career in politics was launched by the great success he achieved in representing the colony at the Halifax Commission of 1877.

THE Morning Chronicle

ST. JOHN'S, TUESDAY, FEB. 5, 1878.

The following is an extract from the letter of a Burin correspondent dated January 26th, 1878 :—

"On Sunday fortnight several American crews, aided by some of our own people, succeeded in hauling many hundred barrels of herring at Anderson's Cove. The people of the place, proof against the Yankee dollar, turned out *en masse*, and having made a successful onset on the Sabbath-violators, cut their nets, traps, and seines in pieces."

The telegram to the Commercial Room yesterday, dated London, February 4, says :—

"A cable dispatch to the *Times* reports that our [Newfoundland] fishermen forcibly prevented Americans from taking bait in Fortune Bay. The matter has been referred to Washington."

A newspaper account of the Fortune Bay incident of 1878.

Sir Sandford Fleming. Born at Kirkcaldy, Fife, Scotland, in 1827, he was chief engineer of the Ontario, Simcoe and Huron Railway, 1857-62, and supervised the building of the Intercolonial Railway after Confederation. He participated in the Washington conference of 1884 which adopted international standard time.

The first Newfoundland railway Act.

CAP. IV.

An Act to authorize the raising by Loan of a Sum of Money for the Construction of a Railway, and for other purposes connected therewith.

[Passed 17th April, 1880.]

than she had received. The determination of this question was eventually referred, under the terms of the Treaty, to a three-man Anglo-American joint commission, which began meeting in Halifax in June 1877. The British appointee to this commission was Sir Alexander Galt, a Father of Confederation. The American member was H.E. Kellogg. The third member, chosen jointly by Britain and the United States, was Maurice Delfosse, Belgium's minister in Washington. The award recommended by Galt and Delfosse but opposed by Kellogg was $5,500,000–$4,500,000 to Canada and $1,000,000 to Newfoundland. The Americans paid up under protest on November 21, 1878.

In the meantime, a sensational press had been given in the United States to the disruption by a group of Newfoundlanders of American fishing operations at Long Harbour, Fortune Bay, on Sunday, January 6, 1878. The Newfoundland government defended the perpetrators of this alleged "outrage" on the grounds that the Americans involved had been clearly violating Newfoundland law in a number of ways. Eventually, Britain paid out $75,000 to the United States in compensation for the Fortune Bay incident. Of this amount, they were able to recover only $17,300 from Newfoundland.

Newfoundland had rejected union with Canada in the 1860s, but in the next decade she sought economic diversification by other means. The great instrument of progress to which she turned was the railway, which had already revolutionized life in much of eastern

C.F. ROWE/EDWARD ROWE

SCENE OF THE HARBOR GRACE TRAGEDY.
ST. STEPHENS DAY DECEMBER 26th 1883.

This lithograph by A.T. Whitman caught two elements of a changing Newfoundland: the persistence of sectarian bitterness, and the coming of the telegraph and railway.

The "Battle of Foxtrap" in 1880 posed an early obstacle to the progress of the railway.

But the minds of the unfortunate people of Upper Gullies and Fox Trap had been poisoned by evil rumours and false stories set afloat by designing persons ; and when Judge Prowse returned to Upper Gullies he found the whole place in commotion—crowds of excited men and women were assembled, threatening violence if the surveyors dared to proceed, and refusing to listen to any explanations. They used the names of two gentlemen of high social standing in St. John's (names at present withheld) who they said had told them to drive off the surveyors, for the Queen was going to give up the country to Canada—that their beds would be taken from them for taxes, and that "a tall gate" (probably "a toll gate") was to be erected at St. John's, and no one allowed to go in or out only by railway.

MORNING CHRONICLE, 29 JULY 1880

North America. The building of the Newfoundland railway was begun in great enthusiasm, but before the eventual western terminus of Port aux Basques was reached in 1897, many careers and reputations were made and broken. In effect, the railway was Newfoundland's first modern economic project and as such gave a foretaste of the sometimes grim realities that would face the colony's twentieth-century would-be developers.

On the return to power of Frederick Carter in 1874, Sandford Fleming, one of the greatest of Canadian railway engineers, was commissioned to survey a route for a line across the island. Fleming's plan envisaged a route far from Newfoundland's established centres of population: from St. John's to Come by Chance, north from there to the Gander River, and then westward to St. George's. The projected cost of the line was a staggering $8.5 million. The conservative Carter did not commit himself to this bold, some said foolhardy, venture; but his successor William Whiteway, who became premier in 1878, seized upon it eagerly, thereby becoming the prototype of Newfoundland's later swashbuckling modernizers. Before facing the electors in 1878, Whiteway got assembly agreement for land grants and an annual subsidy to any company equal to the task at hand. These, of course, were the traditional means by which nineteenth century governments throughout British North America joined with capital on the slippery ground of railway construction.

Sir Robert Thorburn. A merchant, he was born in Scotland in 1836 and died in St John's in 1906.

Richard V. Howley. Newfoundland's rights in the Bait Act controversy were vigorously championed in the journal *Month* in 1887 by this gifted Roman Catholic priest, a member of one of the colony's leading literary families.

Enacting Clause.

No person shall export, haul, catch, or take for exportation, Bait fishes, unless a license has first been granted by the Receiver General.

Be it therefore enacted by the Governor, the Legislative Council and Assembly, in Legislative Session convened, as follows :—

I.—No person shall

(1.) Export, or cause or procure to be exported, or assist in the exportation of, or

(2.) Haul, catch, purchase, or sell for the purpose of exportation, or

(3.) Sell or purchase for the purpose of sale, any Herring, Caplin, Squid, or other Bait Fishes, from, on, or near any parts of this Colony or of its Dependencies, or from or in any of the Bays, Harbors, or other places therein, without a special license, in writing, obtained from the Receiver General of this Colony ; which license may be in the form set forth in the Schedule hereto annexed, and shall be of no avail beyond the fishing season for which it is granted.

Part of the controversial Bait Act of 1886. When the imperial government refused to sanction it, the Newfoundland legislature passed another such act in 1887, this time with the eventual consent of Whitehall.

"Admiral" Prowse attempts to enforce the Bait Act.

A RUDE REPULSE.

A DISCOURAGING report was in circulation here yesterday to the effect that the second ship of Admiral Prowse's squadron received a rather rude repulse from the fishermen of the outer harbors of the Bay where it was cruising. The Admiral himself, it is said, took up a *safe* position well inside at the head of the same Bay, where he could be secure from the effects of the active and *somewhat dangerous* hostilities that were going on outside. It is stated by those who credit the Admiral with the possession of courage that his position is only a piece of strategy on his part, and that he stationed himself there in order to watch the movements of the bait fishermen residing thereabout.

In 1879 Whiteway made what would become a characteristic journey for Newfoundland political leaders – to seek outside help for his grand design. Whiteway's supplication was made in London. He was refused. Lacking the finances to go it alone, and facing a further obstacle in imperial nervousness about any railway construction near the French Shore, Newfoundland retreated. Whiteway would begin, not with a triumphant dash to the west, but with a more modest east coast route, connecting St. John's and Hall's Bay, some 560 kilometres.

His revised plans were given legislative expression in the Railway Act of 1880. A $5-million loan was to be obtained, and the start-up was to be superintended by railway commissioners. In 1881 the government signed

a contract with a New York syndicate spoken for by A. L. Blackman. This contract spawned the Newfoundland Railway Company, which undertook to complete the line to Hall's Bay in five years, with a connecting spur to Harbour Grace. The attendant benefits to the company were the usual grab-bag of subsidies, land grants, loans, and exemption from duty.

Track was at last laid, but by the end of 1882 it extended only a disappointing seventy kilometres from St. John's. In the meantime, Blackman and his cohorts had incorporated the grandiose Great American and European Short Line Railway, reviving thereby the notion, put forward first by Sandford Fleming, of a through line across Newfoundland that would form part of a rapid transatlantic transportation system. An

An English view of Newfoundland's assertiveness in the lobster controversy with France.

"THAT CON—FOUNDLAND DOG!"

JOHN BULL. "IF I COULD ONLY GET HIM TO STAND STILL, I COULD SOON SETTLE THE LOBSTER!"

PUNCH, 4 APR. 1891

PANL/A12-149

Sir Robert Bond. Born in St. John's in 1857, he built up an estate at Whitbourne, which he called "The Grange". Premier from 1900 to 1909, he was one of Newfoundland's foremost statesmen. He died at Whitbourne in 1927, leaving his estate there "to the people of Newfoundland as a Model Farm forever."

James Gillespie Blaine, the American Secretary of State with whom Bond negotiated in 1890. The portrait is by Napoleon Sarony.

SMITHSONIAN INSTITUTION

ancillary project of some of the backers of this venture was a drydock in St. John's, again to be built with government assistance. Whiteway won another election victory in 1882, but the opponents of his railway and other expensive development schemes were now grouped in a potentially powerful new party. When the Newfoundland Railway Company reached Harbour Grace in 1884 only to become bankrupt, their cause quickened.

In the mid-1880s sectarian, railway, and fishery politics, a heady mix, bubbled over. On December 26, 1883, a confrontation at Harbour Grace between Catholics and members of the Orange Order (whose first lodge had been established in Newfoundland in 1863) resulted in five deaths. The ultimate effect of this Harbour Grace "affray" was to split the House of Assembly early in 1885 along Protestant-Catholic lines. Whiteway was now separated from his Catholic supporters, and in October 1885 he resigned as premier in favour of Robert Thorburn, a stern critic of his free-spending policies.

In the election which followed Thorburn rode the Protestant horse to an easy victory, ably assisted by the Grand Master of the Orange Order, Attorney General James Spearman Winter. Having won, he forthwith picked up the thread of denominational conciliation, formed a coalition with the Liberal-Catholic opposition, and concentrated on policies of economic conservatism and retrenchment. His government initially refused further expenditure on the Hall's Bay line.

Newfoundland's flirtation with America, as seen by one British cartoonist.

TRYING IT ON.

Miss Newfoundland.—HOW SHOULD I LOOK IN STARS AND STRIPES?

M. HARVEY, NEWFOUNDLAND (1902)

Sir Robert Gillespie Reid. Born in Scotland in 1841, he became a prominent and wealthy railway contractor and worked on the building of the C.P.R.

More spectacularly, it pushed through, despite great misgivings in London, a draconian Bait Act in a renewed attempt to reduce competition from the French fishery at St. Pierre by cutting it off from its south coast suppliers. For her part, France now claimed that Newfoundland lobster operations were disrupting the fishing activities of her nationals on the French Shore.

Ultimately, Thorburn was drawn willy-nilly towards Whiteway's more expansive ways. Expenditure on a branch railway line to Placentia was the price of Catholic reconciliation in 1886; and in 1888, with an election approaching, the Hall's Bay line was revived. When the votes were counted in November 1889, however, it was Whiteway, the original architect of progress, now calling himself a Liberal, who carried the day. His new administration, which included the able Robert Bond as colonial secretary, struck out in bold new directions, having to cope in the process with the devastation of the great fire which swept through St. John's on July 8, 1892. The railway policy of the new government led to a contract in 1890 with the Canadian promoters Robert G. Reid and G.H. Middleton for the completion of the main line, under new financial arrangements. In 1893 the Hall's Bay terminus was abandoned and Reid, having parted company with Middleton, now agreed, in return for the same monetary compensation, to turn westward at the Exploits River and push on across the island to Port aux Basques.

There were also important new stirrings on the

C.F. ROWE/EDWARD ROWE

PANL/B3-218

Sir James Spearman Winter. He was born in Lamaline on the Burin Peninsula in 1845; he was thus the first outport-born premier of Newfoundland, though his professional career was that of a lawyer in St. John's.

Notes issued by the two banks that failed on "Black Monday," December 10, 1894.

diplomatic front. In 1883, using an escape clause in the Treaty of Washington, an indignant United States had moved to terminate the treaty's fisheries articles, a change that became effective in 1885. A new round of Anglo-American negotiations followed, but the agreement reached was refused ratification by the U.S. Senate. Newfoundland now decided to go it alone in trade and fisheries negotiations with the United States, an option that had first been mooted in 1885. The policy seemed destined for quick success when in 1890 Bond met in Washington with secretary of State James Blaine. The agreement they proposed was, however, strongly opposed by Canada and was in consequence overruled by the imperial government.

The use of the imperial veto in this fashion strained Newfoundland's relations with Canada. Yet this dra-matic series of events was, ironically, to be followed in short order by the only open negotiations for Newfoundland's entry into the Canadian Confedera-tion which occurred between the Colony's rejection of union in 1869 and the local Confederate success of 1948. What brought a Newfoundland delegation to Ottawa in 1895 seeking terms of union was a serious but short-lived financial crisis which struck the colony in Decem-ber 1894, on the failure of the Union and Commercial banks. The 1895 negotiations were carried on in Ottawa with the tottering Conservative government of Sir Mackenzie Bowell. Not surprisingly, the talks failed; and when Newfoundland secured a timely loan in London, relations with Canada slipped back into their traditional groove. The events of 1894-95 did, however, have one lasting effect: Canadian banks

SCHEDULE A.

THIS AGREEMENT, made and entered into at Saint Agreement. John's, in the Colony of Newfoundland, this third day of March, A. D. one thousand eight [L. S.] hundred and ninety-eight, between His Excel-lency Sir HERBERT MURRAY, K.C.B., Governor H. MURRAY, of this Island of Newfoundland and its de- Parties. Governor. pendencies, in Council, hereinafter called "the Government," of the first part; and ROBERT GILLESPIE REID, of Montreal, in the Dominion of Canada, Railway Contractor, hereinafter called "the Contractor," of the other part; Witnesseth, that in consideration of the grants, subsidies, covenants, provisions and conditions hereinafter contained and provided on the part of the said parties respectively, to be made, paid and performed, the said parties mutually cove-nant and agree as follows :—

The preamble to the Act embodying the Reid contract of 1898.

Bishop (later Archbishop) Michael Francis Howley. He was born in St. John's in 1843, and became Roman Catholic Bishop of the diocese in 1894. Like his brothers Richard and James, he had wide-ranging intellectual interests. A Newfoundland patriot, he also had a keen eye for politics.

moved into Newfoundland. Thereafter, the Newfoundland banking system became a branch of Canada's, and the Bank of Montreal became banker to the Government of Newfoundland.

In 1894 Whiteway had given way as premier to A. F. Goodridge, and he in turn to D. J. Greene. Back in office in 1895, Whiteway lost at the polls in 1897, the year the railway reached its western terminus. The Liberals were turned out amidst continuing commercial depression and mounting public debt. Whiteway's Tory successor was Winter. His solution to Newfoundland's public finance problems was to unload the railway albatross. This he attempted to do in a controversial contract made with Reid in 1898, wherein the latter agreed to run the railway for fifty years in return for additional land, together with new financial and proprietorial concessions. Bond launched a vigorous campaign against this arrangement and had strong support from both Governor Sir Herbert Murray and the Roman Catholic bishop of St. John's, Michael F. Howley.

In 1900 the government was beaten in an assembly vote and Bond came to power, making a deal in the process with Edward Morris, the latest darling of the St. John's Irish. Although a supporter of the Reid contract, Morris was willing to temporize for political gain. Having achieved victory at the polls in the same year, Bond set out to modify the deal with Reid. This he did in 1901, bringing to a close an episode of shrill rhetoric about Newfoundland's resources and the role in the colony of outside developers, a theme that would have many echoes in the future.

A.B. Morine auctions the Newfoundland Railway. Born in Nova Scotia in 1857, Morine, a lawyer and journalist, had a colourful career in Newfoundland politics. A member of the Winter government, he was close to Reid and a strong supporter of the 1898 contract. The other figure in the cartoon is probably Edward Morris, who supported the deal Winter proposed. Newfoundland is represented by the sheep. The scene occurs in front of the Colonial Building.

CNS/MUN/WHITEWAY COLLECTION

Nearly a City

Administratively, the highly centralized system that had characterized Newfoundland in the era of representative government was maintained, with some modification, after 1855. Government, of course, affected day-to-day life very little, especially in the outports, but to the extent that it did, the directions came from St. John's. Elective local government did not take hold in Newfoundland; and even St. John's, the largest center of population by far, entered the railway age without it.

There were many reasons for this. In the outports, extended familial arrangements made some of the usual government services irrelevant. Moreover, the ocean resource on which the outports depended was open to all comers and did not afford the traditional property basis for local taxation. Newfoundlanders looked away from their island in regional pockets, and their collective life was something of a paradox: an intense localism, combined with a hierarchy fixated on the capital. The House of Assembly was the cockpit in which this contradiction was resolved – to the extent that it could be resolved – and the outport member was there from its foundation in 1833 to ensure that his locality got its fair share of whatever was on the go.

St. John's was in a very different position. Its urban problems were manifest throughout the nineteenth century – especially its need for fire protection, sanita-

The Act that created the St. John's Municipal Council.

> 50   Ch. 5.   *Municipal Act*, 1888.   51 Vict.
>
> The control of local affairs to be vested in a Board to be called " The St. John's Municipal Council.
>
> I.—The control and management of the local affairs hereafter more specifically set forth, of and pertaining to the Town of St. John's, within the limits hereinafter defined, shall, from and after the First day of October next, be vested in a Board of seven members, to be called "The St. John's Municipal Council," and in this Act hereinafter described as "The Council."

James Goodfellow, first Chairman of the St. John's Municipal Council. Born in Scotland, he was a director of the Commercial Bank, St. John's, 1881-8, and President of the General Water Company, 1887-8. He was a government appointee to the new Municipal Council in 1888, but was elected for Ward 3, 1892-8.

The first steam fire-engine in St. John's, 1885.

tion, and adequate water supply – and various attempts were made to solve them. The result was a unique municipal system, a public-private hybrid in which voluntarism and denominationalism figured prominently.

One seeming limitation on the progress of St. John's was the ownership of much of the town's land by absentees unwilling to be taxed for local improvements. Another was the jealousy of outport members of the House of Assembly about spending that was either primarily or exclusively for the benefit of the capital. But most influential was the attitude of the town's – and Newfoundland's – big merchants, holed up in their enclave on the south side of Water Street. They were determined not to be taxed by the landless

St. John's mob, and they looked to the legislature, especially the appointed Upper House, for what they needed by way of municipal service.

The changes made in Newfoundland's public administration in the second half of the century were shaped by these pressures. In 1855 the Little government created a Board of Works to manage most public property, including streets and roads. In 1859 the General Water Company was formed in St. John's to improve the town's water supply. This company absorbed the holdings of the earlier St. John's Water Company and was empowered to collect an assessment based on the rental value of property. In effect, this was local taxation by private rather than by public means.

PANL/B4·25

St. John's, c. 1890

In any event, this company succeeded and in June 1862 a main was completed from Windsor Lake, an abundant source of water that still supplies part of St. John's. A new sewerage act was then passed in 1863, and debentures due in 1888 were issued under its provisions. As the latter date approached, Whiteway proposed new arrangements for St. John's, both to spread the burden of debt and to effect further civic improvements. After 1888 many St. John's services were administered by a board, known as the St. John's Municipal Council, which included two appointees of the colonial government and five members elected triennially on the basis of a ward system and a complex property franchise. All this gave a new dimension to the already rich political life of the capital, but St. John's was not yet a city, not yet incorporated, and still firmly under the thumbs of the gentlemen who inhabited the Colonial Building.

St. John's, c. 1890, showing hay-carts on Duckworth Street. Though a sizeable town, St. John's still retained its old village ways.

PANL/B4·49

St. John's, seen from the East End, after the fire of July 8, 1892.

By the end of the century, St. John's, long known for its commercial, political, and professional life, was becoming a center of small industry.

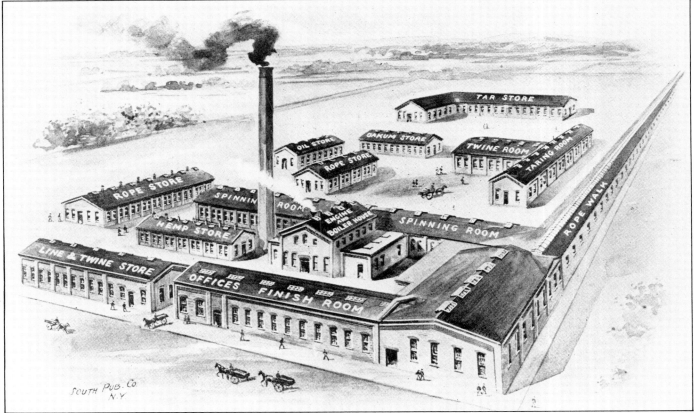

HARVEY, NEWFOUNDLAND (1902)

William Gilbert Gosling. Born in Bermuda in 1863, he worked in St. John's with Harvey and Company. An author, he published *Labrador: its Discovery, Exploration, and Development* (1910) and *The Life of Sir Humphrey Gilbert* (1911). He served as chairman of the commissions that replaced the St. John's Municipal Council, 1914-16, 1920-1, and was mayor, 1916-20. His reforming zeal led to many social and public health improvements in the town and to the passing of a new St. John's Act in 1921.

The dry dock, St. John's. The original construction of this facility, which drew on Newfoundland's still largely maritime economy, dates from 1884.

Michael Patrick Gibbs, Mayor of St. John's, addressing a Labour Day crowd, August 18, 1909. Gibbs was born in St. John's in 1869, and was secretary of the Tenants' League in 1892. A lawyer, he was known as a champion of the working man. He was mayor from 1906 to 1910.

Bond and Morris

IN AUGUST 1902 Premier Robert Bond renewed negotiations for reciprocity with the United States, this time with Secretary of State John Hay. Agreement was quickly reached, but now the bugbear was not Canada – which protested to Great Britain in vain – but fishing concerns in Gloucester, Massachusetts, which were fearful of the impact that an agreement with Newfoundland would have on their own industry. Gloucester had a powerful spokesman in the U.S. Senate in Henry Cabot Lodge, the chairman of the Foreign Relations Committee. Lodge kept the proposed agreement tied up in this committee until January 1905 and then recommended a revised document, which Newfoundland could not accept.

In the meantime, Bond had won another election and in 1904 had accepted, on behalf of Newfoundland, an agreement between Great Britain and France which settled the ancient French Shore question. This arrangement was part of the famous Anglo-French *Entente Cordiale* and augured well for Newfoundland's future. Emboldened by these successes, Bond took on the Americans who had opposed the agreement he had negotiated with Hay and tried to force them into line by limiting the lucrative American herring fishery on the west coast of the island. In 1905 he amended the Foreign Fishing Vessels Act of 1893, thereby jeopardizing the mutually advantageous arrangement between

Sir Cavendish Boyle, governor of Newfoundland, 1901-4. His name is remembered through a much fought over hockey prize, the Boyle Trophy, and for his authorship of the much loved "Ode to Newfoundland."

PANL/B-98

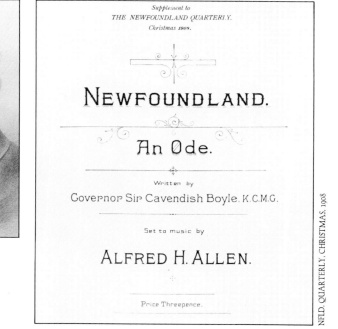

Supplement to
THE NEWFOUNDLAND QUARTERLY.
Christmas 1908.

NEWFOUNDLAND.

An Ode.

Written by

Governor Sir Cavendish Boyle, K.C.M.G.

Set to music by

ALFRED H. ALLEN.

Price Threepence.

NFLD. QUARTERLY. CHRISTMAS. 1908

Newfoundland's surging nationalism at the turn of the century found expression not only in this "Ode," but in an outburst of literary enthusiasm in a variety of genres. A focal point for this activity was the new journal, the *Newfoundland Quarterly*, founded in 1901, from which this title-page is taken.

SMITHSONIAN INSTITUTION

John Hay, by Sir Leslie Ward ("Spy"), 1897.

SMITHSONIAN INSTITUTION

Henry Cabot Lodge (1850-1924), by John Singer Sargent.

visiting American vessels and Newfoundland fishermen in Bay of Islands and Bonne Bay. In addition, Bond advanced a new interpretation of the Convention of 1818, offering a much narrower definition than had hitherto prevailed of American fishing rights in Newfoundland territorial waters.

Great Britain, anxious to improve its relations with the United States in a period of growing international tension, reacted coldly to Bond's scheme, which also faced great opposition among residents on the west coast of the island. Consequently, Bond had to back down and in effect to accept the *status quo ante* with respect to the local American fishery. Thereupon, an Anglo-American agreement referred all outstanding questions under the Convention of 1818 to arbitration by the Hague Tribunal, which rendered its judgment in 1910.

The political price Bond paid for this failure was great. In 1907 Edward Morris broke with him, eventually forming a People's Party. The election which followed in 1908 produced a tie, but Morris, with a sympathetic ear at Government House, won out in the byzantine post-election manoeuvring, became premier in March 1909 and won the ensuing election in May.

A two-masted schooner from Gloucester, Mass., off the Newfoundland coast.

PANL/A17-96

Committee of the Cabot Club, Boston, in charge of an old home week excursion to Newfoundland, 1904. By 1920 every state of the Union had Newfoundland-born residents.

PANL/C1-119

Anti-Bond posters, election
campaign of 1908.

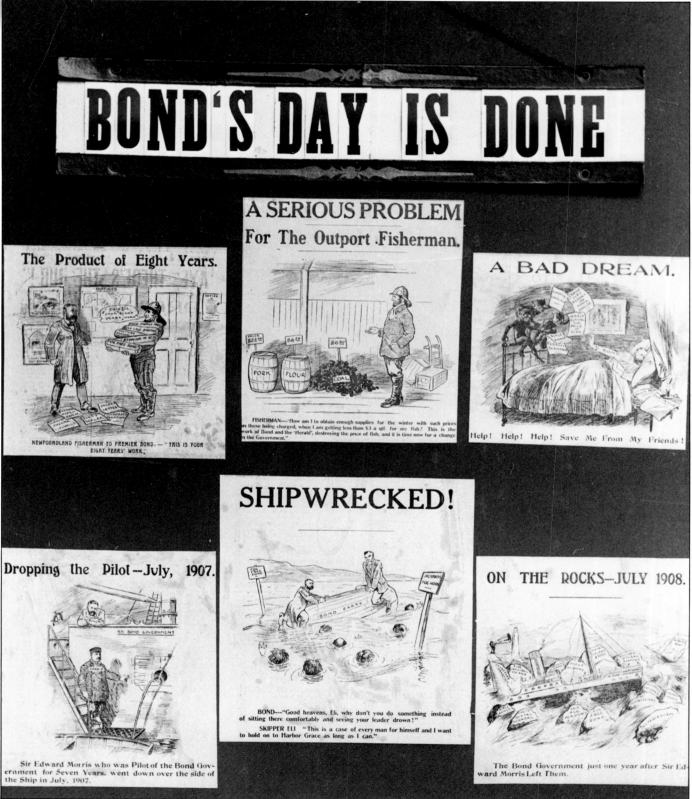

Robert Bond's moment of triumph in 1904, and the removal of a long-standing irritant in Newfoundland's international relations.

EVENING HERALD. 22 APR. 1904

AN HISTORIC OCCASION.

THE PREMIER PRESENTS

The New Anglo-French Treaty

In an Eloquent And Convincing Speech.

PANL/B1-101

NFLD. QUARTERLY. MAR. 1905

Edward Patrick Morris, 1st Baron Morris. He was born in St. John's and was the member of the House of Assembly for St. John's West, 1885-1917. Created a Baron in January, 1918, he died in London in 1935.

Sir William MacGregor, governor of Newfoundland, 1904-9, a key figure in the constitutional crisis of 1908-9. Following the tie election of 1908, Bond, in February, 1909, requested that the new House of Assembly be dissolved on March 25, when it was scheduled to open. His request was denied by the governor, whereupon Bond resigned and Edward Morris was sworn in as premier. When the House

finally met on March 30, it could not elect a speaker. Morris then obtained the dissolution which had been denied Bond and, with the advantage of incumbency, won victory at the polls in May.

The 1908 election ends, and the constitutional crisis begins.

THE EVENING HERALD

PRESCOTT ST., ST. JOHN'S, N.F.

J. T. LAWTON . . . . Editor.

W. J. KENT . . . . . . Business Manager.

The Complete

Election Returns.

THE RESULT 18 TO 18.

EVENING HERALD. 11 NOV. 1908

Transportation and Communication

IN THE SECOND HALF of the nineteenth century, the global revolution in transportation and communication drew Newfoundlanders close to the mainstream and brought them to the attention of the larger world. In the early 1850s the Englishman Frederick Gisborne planned the laying of an underwater telegraph cable across the Cabot Strait. His project failed financially, but it was taken up by the celebrated American Cyrus W. Field, who succeeded in laying the cable in 1856. A line was completed across Newfoundland that same year; St. John's had instant communication with New York.

Field now moved on to the work that would immortalize him – the laying of a transatlantic cable. In 1857 two attempts were made, using the U.S.S. *Niagara* and H.M.S. *Agamemnon*, but both failed. The following year three more attempts also failed, but on the sixth try Valentia, Ireland, and Bull Arm, Trinity Bay, were linked, only to have the cable go dead within two months. The American Civil War now intervened, but a further attempt, also unsuccessful, was made in 1865 using the *Great Eastern*, a marvel of the iron age. Field's triumph came at last in the summer of 1866, at Heart's Content, Newfoundland. The world stood still.

Locally, June 29, 1882, marked another notable beginning, when the first excursion train ran from St. John's to Topsail. As the railway snaked its way north and then west, despite the many shifts of fortune that

Landing the Atlantic cable at Heart's Content, Trinity Bay, 1866.

The first excursion on the Newfoundland Railway, St. John's to Topsail, June 29, 1882.

attended its construction, Newfoundlanders began to move more freely about their island home. Beginning in 1898, it was possible to cross Newfoundland by scheduled train service and connect with the Reid-owned S.S. *Bruce* for North Sydney. In St. John's, service on a street railway was inaugurated on May 1, 1900. The following year the Italian inventor Guglielmo Marconi arrived in St. John's and, to the wonder of the world, received on Signal Hill a wireless message – the letter S – from Poldhu, Cornwall, England. E.J. Pratt called it "one of the big moments of existence."

R. G. Reid's master railroad builders, who supervised the building of the line and its early maintenance. Front row, A. Graham, Alex Cobb, T.P. Connors, D. Steel, D. Ferguson; back row, Barton (possibly), Otto Emerson, J.P. Powell, P.D. Park.

Laying track for the Newfoundland Railway, 1890s.

The S.S. *Bruce* arrived in Newfoundland in 1897 to commence scheduled ferry service on the Port aux Basques-North Sydney run. She was lost in ice in 1911.

Milk delivery by double dog team, St. John's East End, early 1900s.

The S.S. *Kyle*, arriving in Newfoundland in 1913 from Newcastle-on-Tyne, where she was built. She was the most famous of the coastal vessels of Newfoundland and Labrador in the twentieth century.

TOM RONAYNE

Guglielmo Marconi (1874-1937), Italian inventor.

PANL/B1-96

Car 1 of the St. John's street railway, Water Street east, c. 1912.

A.C. HUNTER LIBRARY/KENNY COLL.

Exploration

THE NINETEENTH CENTURY was an age of discovery in Labrador, as curious men, running out of frontiers to explore elsewhere, plunged into the interior of a peninsula known only to the Naskapi-Montagnais. In January 1838 the Hudson's Bay Company employee John McLean and four companions set out overland for Lake Melville from Fort Chimo on the Koksoak River near Ungava Bay. They reached their destination in six weeks, after great hardship.

The following year McLean and eleven others went by canoe up the George River and, pushing overland, he reached Petitsikapau Lake in mid-August, after excr-

uciating labour and prolonged torture by mosquitoes. Leaving the site immediately for the coastline, McLean found his way downriver blocked by one of the world's great cataracts, the Grand (now Churchill) Falls. His book describing his experiences, published in 1849, whetted the appetites of subsequent explorers; to see the "stupendous falls" pictured by McLean became one – but by no means the only – object of late-century Labrador adventurers.

Despite a number of attempts, this was not accomplished until 1891, when Austin Cary and Dennis Cole, two students on an expedition from Bowdoin College in Maine, reached the falls on August 13, having proceeded upstream from the coast. Three weeks later another group arrived at the falls, and within four years

John McLean (1798?-1890), Scottish-born explorer of Labrador.

Dennis Cole and Austin Cary, on their return from the Grand Falls, 1891.

Two Naskapi Indians, Otelne and Arkaske, sketched by William Hind, brother of Henry Youle Hind. In June, 1861, H.Y. Hind, a professor of biology and chemistry at Trinity College, Toronto, led an expedition up the Moisie River, on the North Shore of the Gulf of St. Lawrence. His plan was to follow a reported Indian canoe route to Hamilton Inlet. The river and terrain presented such difficulties that the trek was abandoned after one hundred and twenty miles. William Hind joined the expedition "for the purpose of making sketches and water-colour drawings of scenery, Indians, and any novelty in the vegetable or mineral world which it might be desirable to transfer to his portfolio."

the Canadian geologist A.P. Low had mapped the length of the Hamilton River, together with the lakes and rivers at its headwaters and part of the great mass of water on the interior plateau, Lake Michikimau.

Although the southern regions of Labrador were now better known, the area roughly northwest of Lake Melville was still largely unexplored by white men. In 1903 the Americans Leonidas Hubbard and Dillon Wallace set out with George Elson, an Indian of mixed blood from James Bay, and attempted a crossing from Grand Lake (an extension of Lake Melville) to Lake Michikimau by way of the Naskapi River. Incredibly, they missed the mouth of the river, proceeding inland on a much smaller, barely navigable stream, and the journey, doomed to failure by this initial blunder,

ended fatally for Hubbard. Two years later his wife, Mina Hubbard, accomplished what her husband had failed to do. As the twentieth century began, Labrador was being conquered; but to this day, northern reaches of this huge land mass remain little known.

Mina Hubbard, wife of
Leonidas Hubbard.

Title-page of Mina Hubbard's
account of her Labrador
expedition.

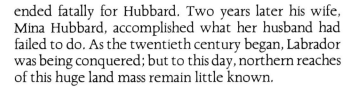

A WOMAN'S WAY THROUGH
UNKNOWN LABRADOR

AN ACCOUNT OF THE EXPLORATION OF THE
NASCAUPEE AND GEORGE RIVERS

BY

MRS. LEONIDAS HUBBARD, JUNIOR

Ellis, Mina Benson (Hubb)

WITH PORTRAITS AND ILLUSTRATIONS

NEW YORK
THE McCLURE COMPANY
MCMVIII

Booming and Mining

THE ATTEMPT TO DIVERSIFY the Newfoundland economy in the latter decades of the nineteenth century was accompanied by many literary flourishes. Enthusiasm over the colony's prospects is reflected in writers such as D.W. Prowse and Philip Tocque, but the island's most prolific boomer was Moses Harvey. In books, articles, pamphlets, and talks, Harvey articulated a vision of a resource-rich Newfoundland with a bright economic future.

These writers found special promise in the government-sponsored geological survey which was started in 1864 under the direction of the Scottish-born Canadian geologist, Alexander Murray. Murray's reports, and those of his successor James Howley, fuelled the expectations of Newfoundlanders, encouraged the idea that a mining boom was imminent, and inspired the belief that the central and western portions of the island had great agricultural potential.

There was much illusion in all this, but mining did at least experience a modest growth, and its long-term future in Newfoundland was indeed great. In 1857 copper was discovered at Tilt Cove, Notre Dame Bay, and mining was eventually started there by Charles Fox Bennett and Smith McKay. Other discoveries followed in this area, and production of copper at Bett's Cove began in 1874. But Newfoundland's first really big mining venture came not in the much-vaunted inte-

Moses Harvey. He was born in Ulster in 1820, and in 1852 became minister of St. Andrew's Free Presbyterian Church, St. John's. His literary and scientific interests were varied, and he was a staunch beliver in progress and a tireless promoter of Newfoundland's development. He had a particular faith in the mineral potential of the colony. He died in 1901.

F.A. ALDRICH

In scientific circles, Moses Harvey was best known for his descriptions of the giant squid or, to use his term, the "devil fish." This 1877 illustration is of the capture of a giant squid at Catalina, Trinity Bay.

PAC/C66125

rior but off the coast, at Bell Island in Conception Bay. Here a huge body of haematite was discovered, and in 1895 a Canadian company began production.

Bell Island became Newfoundland's first real company town, the supplier of iron ore, not only to the emerging Nova Scotia iron and steel industry, but in time to many overseas producers. At Bell Island the picks and shovels were wielded by Newfoundlanders, but management drew much of its talent from elsewhere, an industrial hierarchy that the colony would not soon escape.

Alexander Murray. Born in Perthshire, Scotland, in 1810, and educated at the Royal Naval College, Portsmouth, he was assistant provincial geologist of Canada from 1843 to 1864. His Newfoundland work – he was known in the colony as "Captain" Murray by virtue of his naval connections – occupied him from 1864 to 1883. He died in Scotland in 1884.

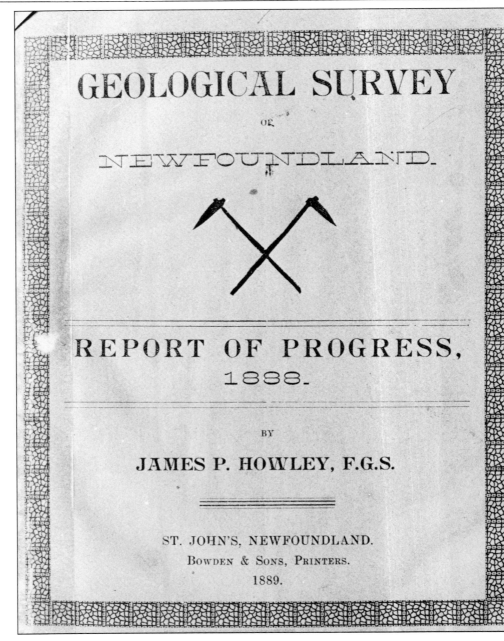

James P. Howley, brother of Archbishop Michael F. Howley and Richard V. Howley. He was born in St. John's in 1847 and was Alexander Murray's successor as head of the Newfoundland geological survey. *The Beothucks or Red Indians of Newfoundland* (Cambridge, 1915), a compilation of authentic reports on this aboriginal people, is his most important publication. He died in 1918.

GEOLOGICAL SURVEY
OF
NEWFOUNDLAND.

REPORT OF PROGRESS,
1888.

BY

JAMES P. HOWLEY, F.G.S.

ST. JOHN'S, NEWFOUNDLAND.
BOWDEN & SONS, PRINTERS.
1889.

The title-page of Howley's 1888 annual report.

An 1883 illustration of the operations at Bett's Cove.

HATTON AND HARVEY, NEWFOUNDLAND (1883)

Miners, Bell Island, Conception Bay. The first mining was a surface operation, but later shafts were sunk beneath the ocean floor, extending by the 1950s some three miles out under Conception Bay.

PANL/A11-55

Old Work and New

If much was changing in late nineteenth-century Newfoundland, much also remained the same. Certainly the fishery, in its many forms, remained the basic industry of the colony. Salt fish was still Newfoundland's principal export product, sent mainly to Europe, South America, and the West Indies – in the face of increasing competition from Norway, France and Iceland.

An important change in the technique of the cod fishery was the introduction of the cod trap in the 1870s. In the seal fishery, a great transformation began in 1863 when the first steamers went to the ice.

Whaling also benefited from this new technology. The greater capitalization now required by sealing entrepreneurs concentrated this business in St. John's, and Harbour Grace went into a marked population decline, a change reflected in the bankruptcy of the once great Munn and Co. in 1894.

Considerable emigration to the United States (especially Boston) and Canada, to which Newfoundlanders had been filtering for a half century or more, was another aspect of this change. The Labrador fishery, however, continued to flourish in Conception Bay and the region benefited greatly from the opening of the Bell Island mining operation in 1895. The contact of Newfoundlanders with Labrador was, of course, still confined to the coast, where the population of Euro-

William Whiteley. Born in Boston in 1834, he built up a large fishing establishment at Bonne Esperance. Known as "Bonay," this port, now in the province of Quebec, was one of the great centers of the migratory Labrador fishery and is remembered in the ballad, "Concerning one Summer in Bonay I spent." The inventor, in 1871, of the cod trap, Whiteley was later a member of the House of Assembly. He died in St. John's in 1903.

PANL/C1-230

Brigus, Conception Bay, a thriving nineteenth century hub of the seal and Labrador fisheries. Its most famous son was Robert Abram Bartlett, who commanded the *Roosevelt* on Admiral Robert Peary's northern expeditions of 1905-6 and 1908-9.

PANL/A1-44

pean descent was still tiny and the only institutional life was confined to the activities of missionaries and the Hudson's Bay Company.

The household economy built around the fishery was complex and employed men, women, and children. Hay was made, vegetables grown, clothing fashioned, nets repaired, berries picked, wood gathered, caplin hauled, fish made, and a multiplicity of other tasks performed in what was now an ancient ritual of work. Newfoundlanders turned their hands to many tasks, often far from home and, as always, with many attendant dangers. Steam power brought greater economy of effort to the seal fishery; but increased competition, forcing all to take extraordinary chances, also brought the possibility of greater disaster, as witnessed

in the horrible *Newfoundland* tragedy of 1914. Such events caused deep stirrings, but while collective worker action was a feature of Newfoundland life by the turn of the century, it still flowed mainly through traditional channels.

In some respects, their versatiliy and itinerant work habits equipped Newfoundlanders well for the inland resource exploitation which their political leaders sought to promote. Take, for example, the pulp and paper industry, which was launched in Newfoundland at Grand Falls by the Anglo-Newfoundland Development Company, formed in 1905. Logging did not need to be a full-time occupation but only one part of a man's cycle of work. This was also the case with the construction gangs which were needed to build the

Tending fish, one of the many tasks performed by women in the outport economy of Newfoundland.

This fine house at Newtown, Bonavista Bay, built by Benjamin Barbour more than a hundred years ago, well illustrates the existence of an outport aristocracy of the sea. The house has thirty-two rooms, including twelve bedrooms. There are five staircases. The Barbour family produced several generations of famous sea captains. In 1932 Captain Job Barbour published *Forty-eight Days Adrift*, an account of an intended voyage, in 1929, from St. John's to Newtown on board the *Neptune II*. Blown by a gale off course, the ship finally reached land in Tobermory, Scotland.

facilities that industry required (the age of hydroelectricity had now also begun in Newfoundland). Newfoundlanders' traditional skills and mobility were readily applied to modern enterprise. Old work in Newfoundland facilitated the new.

Newfoundland sealers at work. An 1883 illustration.

Whale processing plant, Harbour Grace, 1908.

Seal pelt processing. Note the
tally on the door.

Big John Abbott, sealer.

Two sealing steamers in the ice
at Harbour Grace, c. 1889.

Funeral procession,
Newfoundland disaster, 1914.
Seventy-seven men from the
sealing vessel the *Newfoundland*
froze to death on the ice in the
spring of 1914. An uproar
followed in the colony, and
there was a public inquiry. The
disaster was a momentous
occurrence in the history of
Newfoundland. Cassie Brown's
Death on the Ice (1972) is a stirring
account of the tragedy.

View of the power house,
flume, and pipe line, Petty
Harbour, c. 1900. This was the
first hydroelectric power
station in Newfoundland. It
was built by the St. John's
Street Railway Company, and
power was first transmitted
from it to the capital on April
19, 1900. Electric lights had gone
on for the first time in St.
John's on October 17, 1885,
from power supplied by a
steam driven generator in a
local bakery.

An early photograph of the Anglo-Newfoundland Development Company's paper mill at Grand Falls, completed in 1909. In a memorable phrase, S.J.R. Noel has called Grand Falls "the first Newfoundland community out of sight and sound of the sea."

One of the Exploits River Lumber and Pulp Company's camps, Botwood, March, 1906.

Uplift

THE LAST DECADES of the nineteenth century and the early years of the twentieth century gave birth in Newfoundland to several movements of moral uplift. The war-cry of General William Booth's army was first pronounced in Newfoundland in 1885 by Captain Emma Dawson, formerly Emma Churchill, a Newfoundland-born resident of Ontario. In time, the bounteous work of the Salvation Army made it one of Newfoundland's principal religious and social organizations.

The revivalist fervour of late-Victorian England also profoundly affected Newfoundland through the career of the medical missionary Wilfred Grenfell, whose destiny was shaped while a medical student by a chance hearing of the famous American preacher Dwight L. Moody. Having worked since 1888 with the National Mission to Deep Sea Fishermen, Grenfell arrived in Newfoundland in 1892, on the very day of the great St. John's fire. His purpose was to inquire into the medical needs of northern Newfoundland. He found his life's calling in this region, and in Labrador, with which his name became almost synonymous.

Grenfell sought to redeem outport life by a combination of Christian simplicity and economic improvement, through co-operation, diversification, and local initiative. He was a prolific and expansive writer and publicist, and his work attracted an international fol-

Emma Dawson (*née* Churchill), the foundress of the Salvation Army in Newfoundland, seen here seated, as a cadet. She was born in Portugal Cove, Conception Bay, and emigrated to Canada. In August, 1885, she married Charles W. Dawson, a fellow Salvationist. While honeymooning in Newfoundland, she launched meetings on Army lines in St. John's, and the following year the movement was officially established on the island.

SALVATION ARMY HERITAGE CENTRE

The Hotel Metropole, a men's refuge run by the Salvation Army in St. John's.

NFLD. MUSEUM/MUN GEOGRAPHY

lowing of willing helpers. Among them was the Canadian-born writer Norman Duncan, who found in the homely virtues of outport Newfoundlanders, and in the titanic figure of Grenfell himself, the humble nobility that an increasingly urbanized eastern North America seemed to be looking for.

A very different approach to the transformation of outport life was revealed in 1908 when, on the day of the election that Robert Bond and Edward Morris fought to a draw, William Ford Coaker launched the Fishermen's Protective Union (FPU) at a meeting in the Orange Hall at Herring Neck, Notre Dame Bay. Born in St. John's in 1871, Coaker had left school at the age of fourteen and had worked successively as clerk, small merchant, farmer, and telegraph operator. He was well read, and became a stirring and fluent writer and orator. Moreover, the diversity of his early working life had given him an intimate knowledge of both the strengths and weaknesses of outport Newfoundlanders. Like Grenfell he found in them his calling, but unlike his English counterpart his recipe for reform included direct political action as well as the building of new social and economic structures from below. His union established a strong basis of support in the northern bays, and in the election of 1913 union candidates won in eight of the nine seats contested. Coaker had become a big figure in Newfoundland politics and his messianism was sending ripples of fear through the old merchantocracy on Water Street in St. John's.

In a different vein, at Easter in 1911 the American

An early building of the Grenfell Mission, used as a residence for hospital staff. The display of Scriptural texts in this fashion was a distinctive feature of the mission.

Wilfred Grenfell, preparing to operate, c. 1900.

Norman McLean Duncan. Born in North Norwich Township, Oxford County, Ontario, he wrote *Doctor Luke of the Labrador* (1904), a novel obviously inspired by Grenfell, and *Dr. Grenfell's Parish* (1905), a book of essays.

Alice Garrigus had opened the doors of the Bethesda Pentecostal Mission at 207 New Gower Street, St. John's. By 1937 her local foundation had grown to forty-eight assemblies. Another great influence on modern Newfoundland had arisen.

PAC/PA128021/NFB

Bust of Sir William Ford Coaker at the site of his tomb at Port Union, Trinity Bay. In Owenite fashion, Coaker sought to embody in Port Union the institutions he believed could transform Newfoundland outport society.

The Telegrapher.

CNS/COAKER PAPERS

Vol. 1.   PORT BLANDFORD, SATURDAY, FEBRUARY 6th, 1904.   No. 2.

The Fishermen's Advocate.

Published in the interest of Fishermen's Protective Union.

Our Motto: "Suum Cuique."

Vol. 1. No. 14.   COAKERVILLE, SATURDAY, APRIL, 23, 1910.   Price— 1 Cent.

PANL

Logo of Coaker's first newspaper, the organ of a telegraphers' union that he established in 1903.

CNS/MUN/JACK MARTIN

The newspaper of the FPU. In an earlier issue the motto had been translated as: "Let each have his own."

The Orange Hall at Herring Neck, Notre Dame Bay, where the Fishermen's Protective Union was founded on November 2, 1908.

CNS/MUN/JACK MARTIN

The flag of the FPU.

PENTECOSTAL ASSEMBLIES OF NFLD.

Alice B. Garrigus, foundress of the Pentecostal Assemblies of Newfoundland. Referring to a Biblical text also used by Laurence Coughlan in 1776, she wrote in 1937 of her early experiences in Newfoundland that many of those who heard her speak were "like the Bereans of old, they searched the Scriptures 'to see if these things were so.'"

Members of the Royal Naval Reserve in a steam launch in St. John's harbour, embarking for England, 1914. Members of this Reserve were the first Newfoundlanders to go overseas in World War I.

CHAPTER FIVE

"Uncontractual Blood"

The Great War, 1914-18

WORLD WAR I shook Newfoundland society, altering many established ways and shattering many lives. As part of the British Empire, Newfoundland was in the conflict from the sounding of "the guns of August" in 1914 to the eleventh hour of the eleventh day of the eleventh month in 1918. For the size of her population and economy, her contribution was great; and the war left many scars.

The first Newfoundlanders to go overseas belonged to the Royal Naval Reserve and fought as an integral part of the British forces. But under the direction of the Newfoundland Patriotic Committee, the colony also set about training and equipping its own regiment, the first 537 members of which left for overseas in October 1914. Its eventual casualties were staggering – at Gallipoli, the Somme, Ypres and Cambrai. On July 1, 1916, the opening day of the battle of the Somme and a date Newfoundland would not forget, the regiment's roll call following a bloody engagement at Beaumont Hamel stood as follows: 233 killed, 91 missing, 386 wounded. This was from a total of 801. The regiment's record well justified the title "Royal," which was conferred upon it during the war.

Maintaining a war effort of this scope placed great strains on Newfoundland's political and social system, especially as the stream of recruits dried up and the prospect of conscription loomed. In 1917, with its parliamentary mandate running out, Morris's administration gave way to a national government in which all parties represented in the assembly had a voice. Morris only nominally led this new government until December 1918 – he was in London almost all the time – and was succeeded as premier by W.F. Lloyd. Coaker's participation in the national government as minister without portfolio greatly compromised his party and movement. He had been a critic of some of the policies followed earlier in the war, but now had to join with former political enemies in forcing compulsory service on a population with sullen and hostile elements. The deed was done in April 1918 and left a long and bitter taste. Like many farmers in Ontario, many fishermen in outport Newfoundland had no heart for Flanders after the catastrophes that had befallen their compatriots since 1914.

Another imposition of the war, also meeting with Coaker's approval, was prohibition. As elsewhere, the conflict gave a fresh justification and a new urgency to this cause. Also in keeping with what had happened elsewhere, the war introduced Newfoundland women to new public roles, including service overseas as nurses. Finally, the war increased the public debt that Newfoundland had already accumulated through her development policies, an increase that would bear bitter fruit in the next generation.

Newfoundland's hero, winner of the Victoria Cross in the Great War of 1914-18, Private T.R. Ricketts, born in Middle Arm, White Bay. The Newfoundland-born John Bernard Croke (he enlisted as "Croak"), who served with the 13th Battalion, Canadian Expeditionary Force, was awarded the Victoria Cross posthumously for action on August 8, 1918.

PANL/C1-231

PANL/B1-199

Officers of the Methodist Guards. This was a church sponsored young men's organization, resembling the Church Lads' Brigade and the Catholic Cadet Corps. All three were oganized along military lines and flourished in Newfoundland before 1914.

PANL/A2-16

Pleasantville, St. John's, training camp of the Royal Newfoundland Regiment.

St. John's crowd watches
volunteers depart, World War I.

Barbed wire, Beaumont Hamel.

Newfoundland ward, Gifford
House Auxiliary Hospital,
Roehampton, London.

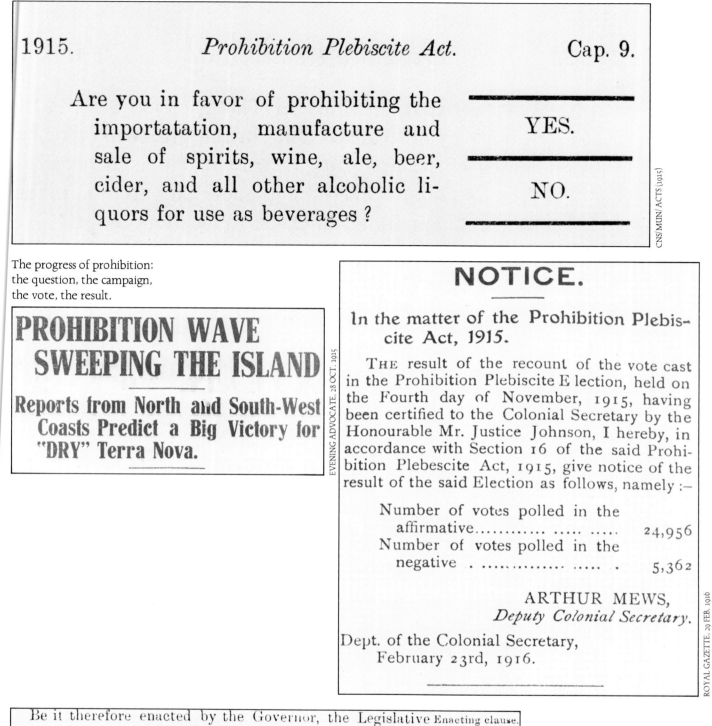

1915. *Prohibition Plebiscite Act.* Cap. 9.

Are you in favor of prohibiting the importatation, manufacture and sale of spirits, wine, ale, beer, cider, and all other alcoholic liquors for use as beverages ?

YES.

NO.

The progress of prohibition: the question, the campaign, the vote, the result.

PROHIBITION WAVE SWEEPING THE ISLAND

Reports from North and South-West Coasts Predict a Big Victory for "DRY" Terra Nova.

NOTICE.

In the matter of the Prohibition Plebiscite Act, 1915.

THE result of the recount of the vote cast in the Prohibition Plebiscite E lection, held on the Fourth day of November, 1915, having been certified to the Colonial Secretary by the Honourable Mr. Justice Johnson, I hereby, in accordance with Section 16 of the said Prohibition Plebiscite Act, 1915, give notice of the result of the said Election as follows, namely :—

Number of votes polled in the affirmative............ 24,956
Number of votes polled in the negative 5,362

ARTHUR MEWS,
Deputy Colonial Secretary.

Dept. of the Colonial Secretary,
February 23rd, 1916.

Be it therefore enacted by the Governor, the Legislative Council, and the House of Assembly, in Legislative Session convened, as follows :—

Enacting clause.

1 The Governor in Council shall, within a period of one month after the date of the passing of this Act, issue a Proclamation in accordance with the provisions of section 17 of the Prohibition Plebiscite Act, 1915, prohibiting the importation, manufacture and sale of intoxicating liquors into or in this Colony at any time after the first day of January, A.D. 1917 ; except as provided in the said Prohibition Plebiscite Act, 1915.

Governor in Council shall issue Proclamation.

DAILY STAR, 18 JULY 1917

The St. John's Daily Star
Newfoundland

VOLUME III.   ($3.00 per Annum)   WEDNESDAY, JULY 18, 1917.   (Price: One Cent)   162

COALITION MINISTRY IS IN OFFICE
Premier Announces New Cabinet And Departmental Personnel To Assembly

Newspaper announcement of the National Government.

Sir William F. Lloyd, Morris's successor as premier under the National Government. Born in Devon, England, in 1864, he was editor of the *Evening Telegram*, 1905-16. He attended the peace conference in Versailles in 1919, and died at St. John's in 1937.

NFLD. QUARTERLY, APR., 1919

ADVOCATE, 15 MAY 1918

THE EVENING ADVOCATE.
Official Organ of The Fishermen's Protective Union of Newfoundland.

Vol. V. No. 107.   ST. JOHN'S NEWFOUNDLAND, TUESDAY, MAY 14, 1918.   Price: One Cent.

GOVERNMENT CONSCRIPTS MONEY AS WELL AS MEN !

William Coaker justifies his support of conscription.

The last desperate attempt to avoid conscription.

EVENING ADVOCATE, 14 MAY 1918

The Real Newfoundland Spirit.

IN THE ABOVE IS PICTURED THE TYPE OF MAN
WITH THE REAL NEWFOUNDLAND SPIRIT
Who went across the seas to fight your battles for you

THIS IS THE TYPE OF MAN
Who Is In Training To-Day.

There is NO YOUNG MAN who has the real good old Newfoundland Spirit, who will wait till he is gone after.

If You Are in Class A,

that is 19 to 25 years of age, and you know you have no good reason for exemption,

You Will Come Before May 25th,

Perhaps your delay has been because the matter has not really been put squarely up to you.

You can take our word for it, that matters are serious, and all Men of Spirit are wanted for the Regiment At Once.

This is a matter of Newfoundland's Honour.

This is a matter of Newfoundland's Life.

You Are a Man of Spirit!
You will Come Now.

THE RETURNED SOLDIERS' AND REJECTED VOLUNTEERS ASSOCIATION.

MRS. GERTRUDE CROSBIE

Ladies' Auxiliary, Great War Veterans' Association, St. John's, c. 1920.

Field-Marshal Earl Haig,
inspecting women, St. John's,
1924. Haig came to
Newfoundland to unveil the
National War Memorial on July
1, 1924.

The main building of Memorial
University College seen here in
1948. The college was founded
in 1925 to commemorate
Newfoundland's dead in the
Great War. The poet Robert
Gear MacDonald wrote this
"Inscription" for it:

Because they rest in grim Gallipoli;
Because they sleep on Beaumont Hamel's plain;
Because beneath the ever-flowing main
Their bodies find a grave eternally
Till the Last Call: in memory of them we,
Whose Land and theirs they saved, that not in vain
Their lives were given, have reared this fitting fane
For many generations yet to be.
Here shall the ancient lore of Rome and Greece,
The learning and the science and the art
Of England, Flanders, Italy and France,
Flow in a stream that plays its generous part
To fertilize the mind of youth, to advance
And foster progress in a world at peace.

The Twenties

BRIEFLY, IN JUNE 1919, Newfoundlanders were distracted from the difficulties of post-war adjustment by one of the great triumphs of the age, the first non-stop crossing by air of the Atlantic, the achievement of the Britishers John William Alcock and Arthur Whitten Brown. But in the decade that followed there were few other encouraging moments.

A political upheaval at war's end brought Richard Anderson Squires to the premier's chair in November 1919, but his first administration faced a difficult export market in the fish trade. William Coaker, as minister of marine and fisheries in the Squires government, made a valiant attempt to reorganize the Newfoundland fishing industry, but the regulations he pushed through in 1920 were eventually abandoned. On the positive side, the government was able to make an agreement in 1923 whereby another paper mill would be started on the island. The developer of the new mill, to be situated at Corner Brook, was the British-backed Newfoundland Power and Paper Company. But this welcome gain was not in itself enough to stop the flow of people from Newfoundland through emigration, which, as the crisis of the fishery deepened, became in some areas a flood.

Economic adversity was accompanied by turbulent, partisan, and vindictive politics. Squires went out of office in July 1923, at the centre of a scandal over the

John William Alcock and Arthur Whitten Brown, in Newfoundland.

The Vickers Vimy biplane of Alcock and Brown, taking off from Lester's field, St. John's, June 14, 1919.

After the landing, June 15, near Clifden in the west of Ireland.

use of public funds in an election held the previous May. Amidst great publicity, the charges against him and some of his associates were subsequently investigated by Thomas Hollis Walker, the recorder of Derby, England.

A period of economic conservatism and retrenchment followed under the premiership of Walter Monroe, a St. John's businessman of the old school. Two achievements of this time were the enfranchisement, in 1925, of women twenty-five years and older, and the great triumph Newfoundland scored against Canada on the Labrador boundary before the Judicial Committee of the Privy Council in 1927.

Newfoundland's ancient claim in Labrador was to the "coast," which in 1763 had been placed under the jurisdiction of the governor at St. John's. A precise definition of this term had become important early in the twentieth century when the interior of Labrador had at last begun to attract the attention of resource developers. In 1920 Canada and Newfoundland had agreed to refer the boundary question to the Judicial Committee of the Privy Council in London. Hence the 1927 decision, which defined Newfoundland-Labrador as the territory within the now-existing boundary. This vast area included in its southern reaches the headwaters of five rivers which flow through Quebec into the Gulf of St. Lawrence: the Romaine, Natashquan, Little Mecatina, St. Augustine, and St. Paul. Thanks to good management and clever argument, a coast had become

Martinside ski-equipped aircraft flown by the Australian aviator Major Sidney Cotton in Newfoundland. The photograph, taken in the immediate post-war period, encapsulates much of the story of Newfoundland transportation.

A 1949 photograph of the Corner Brook Paper mill, built 1923-5. Squires made much of his success in putting "the Hum on the Humber," the river on which Corner Brook is situated.

Sir Richard Anderson Squires. Born in Harbour Grace in 1880, a lawyer, he was premier of Newfoundland, 1919-23, 1928-32. He died in St. John's in 1940.

an empire. Quebec balked, but Newfoundland possessed.

In the election of 1928 the durable Squires made his way back to power, only to fall victim to the Great Depression which began the following year. One wit has said that the depression was hardly noticed in Newfoundland because it came at the end of hard times; but nothing that had happened in the 1920s matched the adversity and humiliation that was in store for Newfoundland in the straitened 1930s. The tidal wave which devastated many areas of the south coast in 1929 presaged a dark decade.

Great hope was placed in William Coaker's regulations to improve the salt fish trade, and their failure to effect lasting improvement marked, in the words of S.J.R. Noel, "the end of Newfoundland's pre-eminence as a fishing country."

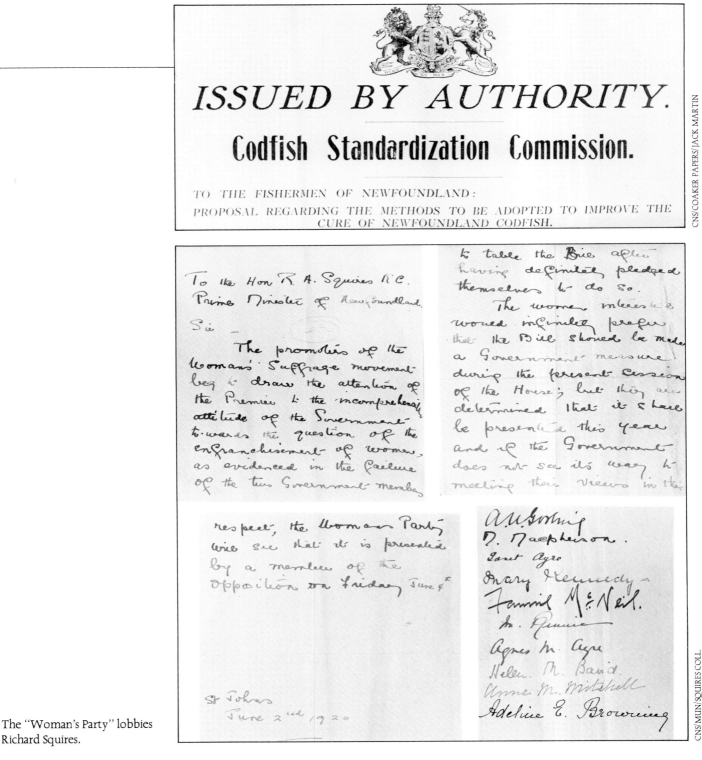

The "Woman's Party" lobbies Richard Squires.

Group of suffragettes, c. 1920. Janet Ayre, one of the signatories of the letter to Squires on June 2, 1920, is holding the banner at the bottom right. Her husband, Eric. S. Ayre, had been killed at Beaumont Hamel, and she is in mourning dress. The War had made rebels of many Newfoundland women, especially those who had gone overseas, moving them to make changes in their world. The suffrage movement in Newfoundland owed much to the upheaval of the War, and in its own fashion was a "testament of youth."

Lady Helena Squires, wife of Sir Richard Squires, the first woman to be elected to the Newfoundland House of Assembly. She was returned in a by-election in the district of Lewisporte, May, 1930. She was defeated in Twillingate in the general election of 1932.

Thomas Hollis Walker. He was nominated by the British government at the request of Newfoundland to investigate allegations against the Squires administration which went out of office in July 1923.

Newfoundland assumed the title of "Dominion" towards the end of the Great War.

Walter Monroe. Born in Dublin in 1871, he was premier of Newfoundland, 1924-8. He died in 1952.

2315

DOMINION OF NEWFOUNDLAND

HIGH COMMISSIONER'S OFFICES.

CABLE ADDRESS.
"RURALITY"

TELEPHONE.
VICTORIA 2302.

58, Victoria Street,
Westminster. S.W.1.

21st January, 1921.

Dear Mr. Squires,

     You asked us some time ago to prepare a digest of the Law of England relating to Women's Suffrage. This digest is now enclosed herewith and I hope it will meet your requirements;

William Warren, premier of Newfoundland (on the right), talks to General Jan Smuts of South Africa, at the Imperial Conference of 1923.

PANL/C1-113

FRANK GRAHAM

Newfoundland team, British Empire Games, Hamilton, Ontario, August 14, 1930. They are, left to right: Greg Power, Bill Cofield, Gerry Halley, Cliff Stone, Ron O'Toole, Sam LaFosse, and Arthur Johnson (Manager). LaFosse, a boxer in the featherweight competition, lost on points to silver medallist Lawrence Stevens of South Africa. "Stevens had a left hand that kept LaFosse out of his range," a newspaper reported, "though the latter was a sturdy youth and absorbed any punishment which the African was able to administer." In the Guinness account of the 1930 games, LaFosse is listed as one of two winners of bronze medals in his weight division.

Sir Patrick T. McGrath. Born in St. John's in 1868, he was trained as a pharmacist but soon turned to journalism, showing great ability in this field. He was Hon. Secretary of the Newfoundland Patriotic Fund during the War, and was a close associate of Edward Morris. A determined and energetic literary digger, he pursued research for Newfoundland's case in the Labrador boundary dispute with vigour, tracking down relevant sources in Great Britain, Canada, and the U.S. He died in 1929.

MUN/JACK MARTIN

Sir John Simon, who, with F.T. Barrington-Ward, W.J. Higgins (Attorney General of Newfoundland), W.T. Monckton, and C.H. Pearson, represented Newfoundland in the Labrador boundary reference to the Judicial Committee of the Privy Council. Newfoundland's solicitors in London were Messrs. Burn & Berridge.

NATIONAL PORTRAIT GALLERY

Canada was represented in the Labrador boundary case by H.P. Macmillan, Aimé Geoffrion, C.J. Doherty, H. Stuart Moore, and C.P. Plaxton. Aimé Geoffrion, shown here, was a leading member of the Quebec bar.

"Labrador," McGrath said on this occasion, "may mean much or little to us according to whether we use or misuse the opportunities it offers for wise and far-seeing exploitation of its dormant resources. My hope is that the information I have supplied to-night may assist this audience and all who read these remarks in reaching conclusions which will strengthen the hands of those in authority, so that this vast possession may be developed, not for the personal profit of mere speculators, but for the abiding advantage of this country and those who dwell in it."

❧ **Labrador and What it Means to Us.** ❧

Lecture Delivered by Sir P. T. McGrath, K.B.E., LL.D., F.R.G.S., at The Pitts Memorial Hall, Monday, 14th March, 1927.

Richard Squires, vindicated at the polls.

First in the Hearts of His Countrymen.

SIR RICHARD SQUIRES BACK TO POWER.

Scene after the tidal wave of November 18, 1929, in which twenty-seven people on the south coast lost their lives.

Downfall

THE DEPRESSION that began with the Wall Street crash quickly overwhelmed Newfoundland's still narrowly based and highly export-oriented economy. Newfoundland's vulnerability to international market forces was Canada's vulnerability writ large. The crisis might be alleviated in Newfoundland, but it could not be solved there. In the circumstances, the government of Richard Squires floundered, attempting even to sell Labrador to Canada to keep its creditors at bay. In April 1932 a mob gutted the House of Assembly. Squires was lucky to escape its wrath, and in the general election that followed his government lost badly and he himself lost in Trinity South. Another defeated candidate was Joseph Roberts Smallwood, who ran in Bonavista South.

Frederick Alderdice, who had succeeded Monroe briefly in 1928, now became premier again. His solution to Newfoundland's mounting deficit – the dominion was having trouble meeting even the interest payment on its debt – was to turn to Great Britain for help. The result was the appointment in 1933, by British royal warrant and with Canadian co-operation, of a commission of inquiry into Newfoundland's future, in particular its financial prospects. The chairman of this body was a Scottish peer, Lord Amulree. The other members were two Canadians, C.A. Magrath and W.E. Stavert.

Governor Sir John Middleton (with hat and cane) and the members and officials of the last House of Assembly of the Dominion of Newfoundland, on the steps of the Colonial Building, St. John's.

Crowd outside the Colonial Building, April 5, 1932.

In its report, the Amulree Commission gave a very unflattering account of Newfoundland's past politics and public adminitration. Its main recommendation was that responsible government be suspended until Newfoundland was again self-supporting. In place of responsible government there would be a commission of government - administration by a governor and six commissioners, all appointed by the government of Great Britain and responsible to the parliament of the United Kingdom through the secretary of state for the dominions. Alderdice's government accepted this plan, as did the Newfoundland House of Assembly, and the new system came into effect in February 1934. It was a humiliation that not even the most hard-pressed of Canada's provinces ever had to endure.

Constitutional change was accompanied by financial help, and the commission of government was able to pay Newfoundland's creditors. It also reformed the public service, established the Newfoundland Ranger force, encouraged the co-operative movement, promoted agricultural settlement, and improved health care, most notably through the establishment of a cottage hospital system in the outports. What it did not do was solve the depression. In 1939 its failings provoked an outburst of criticism from one of its original members, when Thomas Lodge published *Dictatorship in Newfoundland*. What put Newfoundland back on the economic highroad was what put Canada there -the boom that began with World War II.

Frederick C. Alderdice. Born in Belfast in 1872, he was managing director of the Colonial Cordage Company. The last premier of the Dominion of Newfoundland, he died in St. John's in 1936.

An end and a beginning.

The cottage hospital at Markland, one of the agricultural settlements promoted by the Commission of Government. Other such settlements were located at Brown's Arm, Lourdes, Midland, Haricot, Sandringham, Winterland, and Point au Mall. By 1938 ten cottage hospitals were in operation, the most remote from St. John's being the one at Port Saunders.

St. John's, Newfoundland,

February 8th, 1934.

and
Dear Sir ——— Madam,—
~~or~~

I have the honour to inform you that the inauguration of the Government-by-Commission for Newfoundland will take place in the Ball Room, Newfoundland Hotel, on Friday afternoon, February 16th, at three o'clock. The Ceremony will be presided over by His Excellency the Governor. Admiral Sir D. Murray Anderson, K.C.B., C.M.G., M.V.O.

Governor Sir D. Murray
Anderson, speaking at the
inauguration of the
Commission of Government,
February 16, 1934.

This co-operative society
opened for trading August 1,
1938.

Edward Russell. Born in Coley's Point, Conception Bay, Russell was educated at Bishop Feild College in St. John's and Memorial University College, where he trained to be a teacher. He was an outport magistrate from 1935 to 1943, when he became Director of Co-operation with the Commission of Government. In this latter role, he made radio broadcasts and published tracts advocating the co-operative approach. He later drew upon his knowledge of outport Newfoundland in his "Uncle Mose" stories. He died in 1977.

Margaret Iris Duley. She was born in St. John's in 1894 and educated there and in London. Her writing career began during the Depression, and the Newfoundland depicted as background in her first three novels reflects the grim experiences of the Dominion during the 1920s and 1930s. Her third novel *Highway to Valour* (1941) is dedicated to Newfoundland, "a country which the author loves and hates." She died in 1968.

Organized in 1935, with its training center at Whitbourne under the direction of an R.C.M.P. Sgt.-Major, F. Anderton, this police force was in effect an administrative arm of the Commission of Government. In addition to police work, the Rangers inspected weights and measures, collected statistics, helped in the distribution of relief, and in general made themselves an indispensable liaison between the government and the people.

Construction at Gander, 1938. In 1936, on the plateau overlooking Gander Lake, work was begun on an airport. The site had been chosen by the British Air Ministry, two of whose officials had been flown over it by Captain Douglas Fraser, a pioneer Newfoundland aviator. The purpose of this proposed new airport was to facilitate experiments aimed at the introduction of regular transatlantic air service. A complementary and initially more important facility for seaplanes was operational at Botwood in 1937.

"Argentia's Smoking Funnels"

In 1914-18 MOST Newfoundlanders and Labradorians had contemplated war from afar; in 1939-45 war came to them. The airplane and the submarine had given their region a position of immense strategic importance, and it quickly became the scene of intense military activity.

At the outset of the conflict, Mackenzie King committed his government to the defence of the area, and Canada eventually assigned land, sea, and air forces to this great work. The first Canadian military personnel went to Gander and Botwood in 1940. In time, both of these facilities were transferred temporarily to Cana-

dian control. Gander and a new airport at Goose Bay, which Canada began carving out of the Labrador wilderness in 1941, were crucial to the Atlantic Air Ferry by which Great Britain was sustained in her darkest wartime hours. The immediacy of the war to Newfoundlanders was underlined by the German submarine raids in Conception Bay in 1942 (directed against the shipment of iron ore from Bell Island) and by the sinking of the Gulf ferry *Caribou* in the same year. Recently it has become known that a German landing was made at Martin Bay in Labrador in 1943 and an automatic weather station established there.

In 1941 Canada named the Nova Scotian, Charles Burchell, her first high commissioner in St. John's.

Vice-Admiral Sir Humphrey
Walwyn, governor of
Newfoundland, on the portico
of the Colonial Building.

Mackenzie King, with walking-
stick, prepares to board
"Liberator" aircraft at Gander,
August 19, 1941, *en route* to
Britain.

Lord Beaverbrook, British
Minister of Aircraft Production,
at Gander, August 23, 1941.

Another important Canadian initiative was the building of Torbay Airport at St. John's. The first planes landed there on October 18, 1941, and in May 1942 Trans-Canada Air Lines inaugurated scheduled service to the capital. A vital link between Newfoundland and the mainland had been forged. In the Battle of the Atlantic, St. John's was one of the Royal Canadian Navy's principal bases of operation, and its "Newfy-John's" nickname captured the affection with which it was held by the thousands of Allied sailors who found in its vibrant wartime life a welcome relief from the hazards of convoy and patrol duty. The novelist Margaret Duley, herself very active in wartime voluntary work, hit the mark when she wrote that there were many Lili Marlenes in St. John's.

The American impact on Newfoundland was, if anything, even more dramatic than the Canadian and British. Subsequent to the famous Anglo-American destroyers-for-bases deal of 1940, the United States obtained ninety-nine year leases to three base sites on the island of Newfoundland. On these she hurriedly built three large establishments: Fort Pepperrell, an army base at St. John's; Argentia and Fort McAndrew, a naval and army facility on Placentia Bay; and an air base, Harmon Field, at Stephenville. January 29, 1941, the day American forces arrived in St. John's on board the troopship *Edmund B. Alexander*, was a red-letter day for Newfoundland.

Newfoundlanders flocked in their thousands to help build and operate the defence facilities which the war

PAC/PA501330/DND

Last group of Lockheed "Hudson" aircraft, *en route* to Britain, Gander, September 24, 1941.

Two Boeing B-17 "Fortress" aircraft of the U.S. Army Air Force, and, at the extreme right, a Douglas "Digby" aircraft of the Royal Canadian Air Force, at Torbay Airport, October 18, 1941, the day landings were first made there. Note that asphalt is still being laid.

PAC/PA501329/DND

necessitated, leaving traditional occupations and ways, and getting a taste for the North American life-style. The war made visible and accessible a social, cultural, and economic alternative which before had only been imagined. It was a revelation. The people of Newfoundland and Labrador could never go back to what they had been.

In 1942, at the height of the defence building boom, about twenty thousand Newfoundlanders were working on base construction; full employment had come with great rapidity, and the contrast with the depression could hardly have been more startling. The commission of government attempted to regulate this boom in order to achieve maximum economic benefit. New policy instruments were required for this

work and, as in Canada, albeit on a smaller scale, government in Newfoundland took on a modern appearance in the 1940s. In 1942, for example, a Labour Relations Office was created within the commission of government's Department of Public Utilities. This office, under the direction of Albert J. Walsh, supervised a national registration for employment supply and allocation purposes. The work of Walsh and his associates also allowed Newfoundland to bargain hard and successfully with Canada when the latter sought Newfoundland contract workers for its own booming wartime industries.

The commission of government avoided conscription during the war, but a volunteer force, together with a forestry corps, went overseas and many local

RCAF officer with walkie-talkie, at RAF Ferry Command office, Goose Bay, Labrador, May, 1943.

The U.S.A.T. *Edmund B. Alexander*.

men enlisted in the armed forces of Great Britain and Canada. Newfoundland women served in the Canadian forces and were drawn farther away than ever before from the old household economy of their region. Newfoundland had been changed utterly by 1945, and her politicians, bereft of a general election since 1932, were raring to go.

Aerial view of the Argentia area, September 25, 1940.

Formation of U.S. Marines, Argentia, February 8, 1941.

Aerial view of the U.S. base at Argentia, April 24, 1942.

The meeting of Churchill and Roosevelt in Placentia Bay, August 10-12, 1941, symbolized Newfoundland's strategic importance in the Second World War. Out of this meeting came the Atlantic Charter. This photograph was taken during church services on the H.M.S. *Prince of Wales* on August 10. Included are, left to right: Harry Hopkins, Averell Harriman, Adm. Ernest J. King, Roosevelt, Gen. George C. Marshall, Churchill, Sir John Dill, Adm. Harold R. Stark, and Adm. Dudley Pound.

View forward over the bows of H.M.C.S. *Vancouver*, *en route* from St. John's to Boston, June, 1945.

The ferry S.S. *Caribou* was torpedoed in the Cabot Strait, in passage from North Sydney to Port aux Basques, October 14, 1942, with the loss of one hundred and thirty-seven lives.

German submarine U-537 at anchor, Martin Bay, Labrador, October 22 or 23, 1943, armed German crewman keeping watch in foreground. The photograph was taken from the eastern shore of the bay, probably some distance south of the site of the weather station which the Germans established there.

Boom defence protecting the iron ore loading piers, Bell Island, Conception Bay, August 9, 1944.

PANL/B1-155

Sir L.E. Emerson, Commissioner for Justice and Defence in the government of Newfoundland, talking to Newfoundland troops in England.

PANL/A12-88

Sir Albert J. Walsh. Born in Holyrood, Conception Bay, in 1900, he was one of two members elected to the House of Assembly for Harbour Main district in 1928, becoming magistrate in Grand Falls in 1935. In 1940 he joined the Department of Justice, and in 1942 was made Labour Relations Officer in the Department of Public Utilities. He became a member of the Commission of Government in 1944, later becoming its vice-chairman. He was the first lieutenant governor of the province of Newfoundland, and later chief justice of its Supreme Court. He died in 1958. Walsh was probably the most important Newfoundland politician of the 1940s.

At the Caribou Club, a social center for Newfoundland forces, London.

Departure of Women's Royal Canadian Naval Service recruits from St. John's, August 29, 1943.

PANL/C1-2

PAC/PA116093/DND

157

Newfoundland women, probably employees at the Dominion Woollens & Worsted Company, Hespeler, Ontario. The Commission of Government imposed special conditions on prospective Canadian employers of female contract workers from Newfoundland.

ATLANTIC GUARDIAN, APR., 1945

Homeland To Hespeler

ifty Newfoundland girls travelled Far to Do War Work in an Ontario

extile Plant, But Today They're Quite at Home in Cozy Winston Hall

Workmen at Goose Bay, May, 1943.

PAC/PA116034/NFB

R.A. MacKay was born in Victoria County, Ontario, in 1894, and was Professor of Government and Political Science at Dalhousie University from 1927 to 1947. From 1943 to 1947 he was special assistant to the Under-secretary of State for the Canadian Department of External Affairs, and in this position greatly influenced policy towards Newfoundland. In 1946 he edited *Newfoundland: Economic, Diplomatic and Strategic Studies*, a work that reflected Canada's involvement in, and knowledge of, Newfoundland and Labrador in the 1940s.

PAC/C5058

Trans-Canada Air Lines crew, St. John's May 1, 1942, the inaugural trip of the new TCA service between Canada and Newfoundland. The crew comprises, left to right: Capt. Burton J. Trerice, Stewardess Dorothy Reid, R.N., and Capt. W.W. Fowler, Operations Superintendent, acting co-pilot. The plane is a Lockheed 14 CF-TCG

AIR CANADA ARCHIVES X13621

PANL/A-7-167

Two Newfoundland loggers in Scotland, World War II. Newfoundland sent foresters overseas in both world wars.

PAC/PA-116901/DND

Children examining anti-aircraft guns of H.M.S. *Newfoundland*, St. John's, August 10, 1944.

Empire Day Parade, St. John's, May 24, 1945.

PAC/PA-116687/DND

Surrendering German
submarine U-190, *en route* from
Bay Bulls to St. John's, June 3,
1945. Photograph taken from
Consolidated "Liberator"
aircraft of No. 10 (BR) Squadron,
RCAF.

PAC/PA110940/DND

PAC/PA128005/NFB

Fort Pepperrell, U.S. Army Base,
St. John's, September, 1948.

PAC/PA128015/NFB

Sundaes at Frost's Restaurant,
St. John's, September, 1951.

One of Ten

IF CANADIANS MADE a great mark in Newfoundland in the 1940s, Newfoundlanders had also made their mark on Canada, as the careers of E.J. Pratt, Silby Barrett, and others showed. The destinies of the two peoples had long been linked, and the War made the bonds between them, administrative and personal, stronger than ever before. But the formal process by which Newfoundland became a Canadian province may be dated from December 11, 1945. On that day, the new Labour Prime Minister of Great Britain, Clement Attlee, announced that an election would be held in Newfoundland to select, constituency by constitu-

ency, delegates to a National Convention. The purpose of this convention would be to advise Great Britain on "possible forms of future government,"among which the Newfoundland people would then decide by referendum.

The election which followed did not stir much enthusiasm; indeed, eight of forty-five delegates were elected by acclamation. The mood of the electorate changed dramatically, however, when the government-owned radio station VONF began broadcasting the Convention's proceedings nightly. On the only item of real business before them – the advice to be tendered the British government – there were deep divisions among the Convention's members. The main one was between those who wanted Newfoundland

E.J. Pratt. Born in Western Bay, Conception Bay, in 1882, he left for Canada in 1907, and published his first major volume of poetry, *Newfoundland Verse*, in 1923. He was by the 1940s one of Canada's leading poets and teachers.

Silby Barrett. He was born in Old Perlican, Trinity Bay, in 1884, and went to Nova Scotia to work as a coal-miner in 1902. He helped to establish the United Mine Workers of America in Nova Scotia, and by the 1940s was a labour leader of national importance.

BELOW
Eugene A. Forsey. He was born at Grand Bank in 1904. In 1935 he was one of the contributors to *Social Planning for Canada*, one of the best known reform documents of the decade. By the 1940s he was one of Canada's leading labour intellectuals, and is shown here in 1949 speaking at a weekend school organized by the Toronto Political Action Committee of the Canadian Congress of Labor.

Joseph W. Noseworthy was born in Lewisporte, Notre Dame Bay, in 1888, and went to Canada in 1910. On February 9, 1942, running as a CCF candidate in the Ontario constituency of York South, he defeated Arthur Meighen, national leader of the Conservative Party.

to return to its pre-1934 constitution and those who wanted Newfoundland to become a province of Canada. The spokesman who emerged to lead the Confederate forces in the convention was J.R. Smallwood, the delegate for Bonavista Centre, who, thanks to his earlier career as announcer on a show he had invented, "The Barrelman," had the best-known radio voice in Newfoundland. This was a valuable asset in a society whose complex traditional culture was still being handed down to an extent by word of mouth.

Smallwood and his Confederate supporters were able to manoeuvre the convention into sending a delegation to Ottawa to see whether suitable terms of union with Canada could be devised. This delegation laboured in the Canadian capital during the summer of 1947 and returned home with the promise of the goods. But the majority of the members of the Convention were not pleased with the result. The crunch came on January 28, 1948, when the vote was taken on Smallwood's motion that Confederation be recommended to Great Britain for inclusion on the referendum ballot. His motion was defeated 29 to 16, whereupon the Convention recommended these choices: "Responsible Government as it existed prior to 1934" and "Commission of Government."

For the moment, the Confederates were stymied, but, happily for them, the Convention was only an advisory body. Smallwood and his associates took their case to the Newfoundland people and, through the Governor, to the Attlee government. Their initiative

Arthur Scammell. Born at Change Islands, Notre Dame Bay, in 1913, he was the author of the famous ballad "The Squid-Jiggin' Ground," which was played on the carillon of the Peace Tower in Ottawa in celebration of Newfoundland's entry into Canada. In the 1940s he was a teacher in Montreal.

ART SCAMMELL

Members of the National Convention who went as a delegation to Ottawa in 1947, with Louis St. Laurent. Included, left to right, are: G.F. Higgins; J.R. Smallwood, secretary of the delegation; T.G.W. Ashbourne; St. Laurent; F. Gordon Bradley, chairman; Rev. Lester Burry, the sole representative in the Convention for Labrador; C. H. Ballam, and P.W. Crummey.

PAC/PA128075/NFB

was politically important, but Whitehall had long since decided, in consultation with Ottawa, that union with Canada would be the best outcome for Newfoundland. Accordingly, the British now ruled that Confederation would be on the ballot after all, along with a revised version of what the National Convention had recommended. In its final form the ballot featured, in order, these choices:

1. COMMISSION OF GOVERNMENT for a period of five years.

2. CONFEDERATION WITH CANADA

3. RESPONSIBLE GOVERNMENT as it existed in 1933. In keeping with another British decision, the legislation governing the vote also required that a run-off between the two most favoured options be held if a

majority was not achieved on the initial balloting. The date for the first referendum was set for June 3, 1948, and the contest which followed was bitterly fought. One interesting feature of it was the emergence on the responsible government side - that is to say, among those who wanted, at least as a first step, to restore the pre-1934 constitution - of a campaign, led by Chesley A. Crosbie, in favour of economic union with the United States. The result, on June 3, was inconclusive; 69,400 supported responsible government, 64,066 Confederation, and 22,311 the continuation of the existing Commission system. The required majority had not been achieved. The run-off between the "high liners" was held on July 22, and produced a Confederate victory - by 78,323 to 71,334.

Reading the news, Corner Brook, July, 1948.

Chesley A. Crosbie. A businessman, he was born in St. John's in 1905. An advocate during the referenda of 1948 of economic union with the United States, he was the only member of the Newfoundland delegation that negotiated the final Terms of Union with Canada to decline to sign them.

Sectarianism, a traditional rallying cry in Newfoundland politics, had become an issue during the referenda campaigns, but its importance in determining the final outcome has been exaggerated at the expense of the great impersonal forces which were pushing Newfoundland in a North American direction. Regionalism was another factor in the final outcome. Thus, in the decisive second referendum, every constituency favouring responsible government was on the Avalon peninsula. This was not only the oldest settled part of Newfoundland but the area of the island most influenced by the St. John's economic élite, some of whose members apparently feared the advent of stronger Canadian business enterprise. Moreover, many people in this part of Newfoundland had close family ties in New England and New York, a connection which the war had reinforced.

On December 11, 1948, the Terms of Union between Newfoundland and Canada were signed in Ottawa. By these terms, Confederation was to become a reality "immediately before the expiration of the thirty-first day of March, 1949." As might be expected, given the close result of the voting, the opponents of Confederation did not accept their defeat lightly, but their appeals to London for redress were brushed aside. The fish had been fried.

Sir Albert Walsh, chairman of the Newfoundland delegation, signing the Terms of Union between Canada and Newfoundland, Senate Chamber, Parliament Buildings, Ottawa, December 11, 1948. Seated with him is Prime Minister Louis St. Laurent. Standing, left to right, are: Hon. Milton F. Gregg, Minister of Veterans' Affairs; Hon. J.J. McCann, Minister of National Revenue; Hon. Brooke Claxton, Minister of National Defence; F. G. Bradley; G.A. Winter; Philip Gruchy; J.R. Smallwood; and J.B. McEvoy.

Hail and Farewell

TOWARDS THE CLOSE of the tumultuous decade of the 1940s, Margaret Duley wrote: "It was a time of mourning indeed, a time for an old-world lament. Everywhere it was change, startling change. Newfoundland would never be the same again. One could hear the old days in recession." Her words were a fitting epitaph for the generation of 1949.

At home on Bell Island, 1949.

The banking schooner *Philip E. Lake*, 1949.

PAC/PA128000/NFB

Making hay, Port de Grave,
Conception Bay, 1953.

PAC/PA128000/NFB

Lumberjack Merril Bennet of
Flat Bay, St. George's Bay, at a
Bowater's camp on the
Humber River, 1948.

A home in Port de Grave, 1949.

Carrying water, Portugal Cove, 1949.

Stanley Bros. general store, Clarenville, Trinity Bay, 1949.

"The Living Fathers of Confederation."

"As Fresh as Dulse"

The Return to Party Politics

On APRIL 1, 1949, the first government of the new province was sworn in, with J.R. Smallwood as premier. As leader of the newly formed provincial Liberal party, he led his followers to victory on May 27, and the Liberals carried five of Newfoundland's seven seats in the federal election that followed one month later.

The province had settled into a political groove from which it would not soon be dislodged. In the 1950s good times continued almost everywhere in North America, and Confederation looked like a big success. Smallwood was associated with its every achievement and came to enjoy great personal power. He won six successive provincial elections and helped his federal allies carry the province in seven successive national contests. He was an unsettling mixture of creativity and conservatism. The former found expression in the many ambitious programs his government launched. The latter could be glimpsed in his approach to politics, which harked back to pre-1934 days. In 1968 his biographer, Richard Gwyn, called him "an unlikely revolutionary," and the description still seems apt. His hold on power has been compared to that of Maurice Duplessis. It has been said of the Quebec leader that he "buried the past" of his province by "perfecting the political techniques of the past." Something like that could be said of Smallwood.

His main opposition came from the Progressive Conservative party, which was built in the province largely on the wreckage of the anti-confederate movement. It won few seats in the 1950s except in St. John's and vicinity, though it did garner 45.2 per cent of the popular vote in the province in the Diefenbaker sweep of 1958. Canada's other parties made little impact on Newfoundland in the short run. A dissident provincial Liberal member declared himself a CCFer in 1955, but neither that party nor its successor, the NDP, won a seat in the province until Fonse Faour's victory in a federal by-election on October 16, 1978, in Humber-

St. George's - St. Barbe. The provincial progenitor of the NDP, the Newfoundland Democratic Party, a labour-based party formed in 1959, won a significant popular vote in the provincial election of that year, but no seats.

Federal-provincial relations during the Smallwood era were generally tranquil, as the new province felt its way along the myriad paths of Canadian federalism. Newfoundland's first representative in the federal cabinet was F. Gordon Bradley. He was succeeded in 1953 by the accomplished Ottawa mandarin, J.W. Pickersgill, who gave the province considerable leverage on the national scene.

The one really sour time in relations between St. John's and Ottawa in the immediate post-Confedera-tion period came in 1959 when two nasty spats developed between Smallwood and Diefenbaker: one involved the use of the RCMP in a savage woodworkers' strike; the other concerned the payments the federal government proposed to make to Newfoundland under Term 29 of the Terms of Union of 1948. This clause had provided for the appointment of a royal commission, within eight years of union, to review Newfoundland's financial position as a province. The commission had been duly appointed in 1957 under the chairmanship of Chief Justice J.B. McNair of New Brunswick, and its recommendations had set the stage for the donnybrook that followed. This split the PC party in Newfoundland and created from its ranks the short-lived United Newfoundland Party (UNP), which

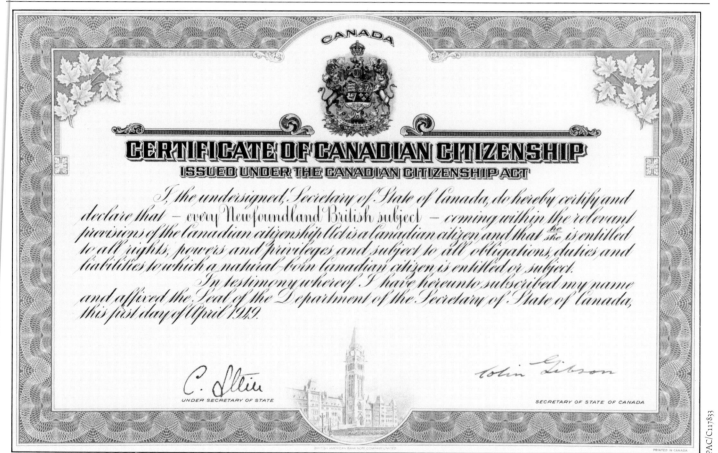

Canadian credentials.

Harry G. Mews, first leader of the Progressive Conservative Party in the province of Newfoundland. He is seen here in 1951 as mayor of St. John's.

contested the provincial election of 1959, winning two seats in St. John's.

Political change in Newfoundland came in the wake of a social and economic transformation. It was signalled by Liberal defeat in a provincial by-election in Gander in 1967 and confirmed by the PC victory in six of Newfoundland's federal seats in the 1968 election, which Pierre Trudeau won handily in the country. Suddenly, Smallwood was fighting for his political life, as the province's emerging middle class, much of it of a new generation, reached for power.

The climax came in the stormy election of October 28, 1971, which produced first an uncertain result, and in time a constitutional crisis. Weeks of partisan strife followed in which Tom Burgess, the only member elected by the New Labrador party (a vehicle for regional grievance), figured prominently. And then, in January 1972, Frank Moores became the province's first PC premier.

In 1979 Moores resigned as party leader and was replaced as premier by Brian Peckford, in some respects a more authentic representative of what the province had become. Moores had scored many points by adopting a more critical attitude to Ottawa; Peckford would give this approach greater prominence.

The advent of the Royal Canadian Mounted Police, which absorbed the Newfoundland Rangers, signalled the extension of Canadian federal authority to the new province. An officer of the force is seen here looking out from a lighthouse at Bonne Bay.

R.C.M.P.

J.R. Smallwood and J.W. Pickersgill campaigning at Musgrave Harbour, June, 1953.

TORONTO STAR/J.W. PICKERSGILL

W.J. Browne. Born in St. John's in 1897, he was first elected to the House of Assembly in 1924. In 1949 he became the member of the House of Commons for St. John's West. Returned to Ottawa in 1957, he became Minister without portfolio in the Diefenbaker government. In 1960 he was made Solicitor-General for Canada. He was the first Progressive Conservative from Newfoundland to sit in the Canadian cabinet.

Ed Finn, leader of the Newfoundland Democratic Party in the provincial election of 1959. Later he worked for the Canadian Union of Public Employees in Ottawa and became a labour columnist for the Toronto *Star*.

Duncan Macpherson's Toronto view of the political slugfest in Newfoundland in 1959.

J.R. Smallwood's last days in office, as depicted by Duncan Macpherson.

Part of the constitution of the New Labrador Party.

CONSTITUTION OF THE NEW LABRADOR PARTY IN
NEWFOUNDLAND AND LABRADOR

ARTICLE 1 - OBJECTS
The objects of the New Labrador Party of Newfoundland and Labrador shall be:
1. To advocate and support the political principals of the New Labrador Party.
2. To develop and determine policy.
3. To organize the New Labrador Party in each district of Labrador.
4. To promote the election of candidates of the New Labrador Party in provincial elections.

Frank Duff Moores, premier of Newfoundland, 1972-9. He is seen here speaking to pupils at Dawson Elementary School, St. John's, during the celebrations in 1974 marking the twenty-fifth anniversary of Newfoundland's entry into Confederation.

Prime Minister P.E. Trudeau and Fisheries Minister Romeo Leblanc in December, 1976, at the conclusion of the negotiations leading to the establishment of the 200-mile limit on Canada's offshore on January 1, 1977.

MUN EXTENSION

FISHERIES & OCEANS CANADA

173

Fonse Faour and Ed Broadbent, national leader of the New Democratic Party, campaigning at Port au Choix, October 7, 1978.

John C. Crosbie. Born in St. John's in 1931, he served in the Liberal government of J.R. Smallwood from 1966 to 1968 and in the Progressive Conservative government of Frank Moores from 1972 to 1976. He was elected to the House of Commons in 1976 and became Minister of Finance in the government Joe Clark formed after the election of 1979. He is seen here showing reporters the mukluks he would wear to give the budget speech which led to the federal election of 1980.

Premiers Peter Lougheed of Alberta and Brian Peckford of Newfoundland, in a helicopter wearing survival gear, 1981. Peckford became the province's third premier in 1979.

NEWFOUNDLAND AND LABRADOR

MANAGING ALL OUR RESOURCES

The cover of a provincial government policy document in 1980. The title caught Newfoundland's ambitions and reflected the tone of her relations with Ottawa in the early 1980s. The provincial flag shown here was adopted in 1980.

Economic

THE PACE OF ECONOMIC DEVELOPMENT in Newfoundland speeded up after Confederation, exhibiting elements of both continuity and change. Like the CCF in Saskatchewan in the 1940s, the Liberal government of Newfoundland in the 1950s tried, with only modest success, to promote small-scale secondary industry. Simultaneously, Smallwood attempted to do what Squires and Whiteway had sought before him – to open up the resources of the country to the international market. His most spectacular efforts were made in Labrador, whose riches technology could now master. In the 1950s mining of iron ore began in western Labrador, the product being shipped to the steel mills of North America and the world via the newly-built Quebec North Shore and Labrador Railway and the port of Sept-Iles on the St. Lawrence.

Then in 1966 work began at Churchill Falls on one of the world's great hydro installations. The political and financial machinations behind the Churchill Falls enterprise were extraordinarily complex, and the arrangements made became the subject of great controversy in Newfoundland after the Progressive Conservatives came to power in 1972. To get the project going, Smallwood had to make enormous concessions, beginning with those he handed to the British Newfoundland Corporation (Brinco) in 1953. In 1969 Brinco's subsidiary, Churchill Falls (Labrador) Corporation

Gordon F. Pushie, Director General of Economic Development for Newfoundland, holds up an oil painting by W.C. Werthman, July, 1953.

Guenther F. Stahl, vice-president and commercial manager of the Atlantic Hardboard Industries Ltd., points to the first "Fibrply" made in the company's plant at Topsail, July 17, 1953.

In Labrador, September, 1949. Examining an iron ore sample are, left to right: Jules Timmins, President, Hollinger Consolidated Gold Mines; Premier J.R. Smallwood; W.H. Durrell; and Jack Little.

(CFLCo) signed a contract with Hydro-Québec for the sale of almost all the power to be produced at Churchill Falls. The prices set in this agreement, scheduled to last for sixty-five years from the effective date (1976), seemed ludicrously low in Newfoundland after the OAPEC oil embargo of 1973 and the increase in world energy prices that followed.

These circumstances brought the province into serious dispute with Quebec. The ambition of the province in this strife was twofold: to revise the terms of the 1969 agreement, and to obtain better terms for the export of any further power developed in Labrador. In 1974 Newfoundland gained control of CFLCo and created the Newfoundland and Labrador Power Corporation – in 1975 renamed the Newfoundland and Labra-

dor Hydro-Electric Corporation – the basis for which had been laid in the establishment of a provincial power commission in 1953. In 1978 the Newfoundland and federal governments formed the Lower Churchill Development Corporation in a new joint approach to the generation of power in Labrador. Overall, Newfoundland's political mastery of Labrador in the first generation after Confederation did not translate into economic hegemony. Quebec had lost the Labrador boundary dispute in 1927, but in the short run at least her geographical advantage ensured that she would reap the greater gain from the opening up of the region.

On the island of Newfoundland itself, mineral and hydro-electric production and ancillary activities also

At mile 12 of the Quebec North Shore & Labrador Railway, near Sept-Iles, Quebec, September, 1952.

John C. Doyle is at the center.

expanded rapidly after 1949, and in 1981 a third paper mill was officially opened at Stephenville, using some of the facilities of an earlier failed enterprise, Labrador Linerboard Limited. Change in the fishing industry was also rapid, and many new techniques of catching fish were introduced. Processing plants were built all around the province. The construction boom that had begun with the war continued thereafter, to the great benefit of local business. Public sector and service employment grew withal. Indeed, governments were prime movers in Newfoundland's economic flowering, as the close association of business and political élites in the province clearly showed.

Needless to say, this major process of economic change caused people to move about in great numbers. The urbanization of Newfoundland had been in progress before 1949; but the provincial government (and, later, the federal government) attempted to encourage this process of "resettlement" with financial support. By the late 1960s they were receiving harsh criticism for their efforts, though not always from ordinary people. Governments also had to deal with the urgent social and economic needs created by the decline of old industrial communities (the Bell Island mines closed in 1966); and they faced similar problems as the American forcees withdrew from St. John's, Stephenville, and Goose Bay, leaving only a skeleton staff at Argentia.

The province's population grew rapidly after Confederation, but despite great economic gains,

Part of the Iron Ore Company
of Canada's operation at
Labrador City.

Newfoundland could still not deliver the goods to all her people. With immigration barriers removed, Newfoundlanders in this period moved in large numbers to the Canadian mainland, especially to Ontario. By 1971 there were 97,485 Newfoundlanders living in the other provinces, 59,585 of them in Ontario. The day of the Newfie joke had dawned.

Victor Young, Chairman and Chief Executive Officer of Newfoundland and Labrador Hydro, making a point about Labrador. Born in 1945, his career exemplifies the growth of local managerial expertise and the importance in the province's economy of the public sector.

Victoria Dam, one of the major control structures in the Bay d'Espoir hydroelectric development. Work on the 600 megawatt Bay d'Espoir development, the largest hydro project ever undertaken on the island of Newfoundland with a drainage area of approximately 1500 square miles, began in 1964. This dam was part of the second phase of the project, which started in 1966.

View of the main control room, Churchill Falls power project, Labrador. According to Newfoundland and Labrador Hydro, in 1981 this project supplied Quebec with 35.9 billion kwh of electricity at an average rate of 2.6 mills per kwh – the equivalent, at then existing prices, of sixty million barrels of oil at a rate of $1.50 per barrel.

Paper machine, Abitibi-Price mill, Stephenville.

DEPT. OF FISHERIES/NFLD.

DEPT. OF FISHERIES/NFLD.

Women processing fish.

Hauling monofilament gill nets with a hydraulic gurdy. The gurdy took much of the back-breaking labour out of the inshore cod fishery.

Crane owned by one of Newfoundland's largest enterprises, and operated by Clarence Butt of Upper Island Cove, Conception Bay. Founded by W.J. Lundrigan, a survivor of the *Caribou* tragedy of 1942, Lundrigan's Ltd. was operating by 1981 as far afield as Saudi Arabia.

MUN EXTENSION

John M. Shaheen, bottom right, president of Shaheen Natural Resources Company, Inc., signs the contract for the charter of Cunard Line's flagship, *Queen Elizabeth 2*, with Richard B. Patton, president of Cunard Lines Ltd. Standing are Homer White (left) and Roy M. Furmark, executive vice-presidents of Shaheen Natural Resources. The ship sailed from New York to Come by Chance, Placentia Bay, with a star-studded passenger list, for the official opening in October, 1973, of the oil refinery, illustrated in the background.

The Marystown Shipyard, a major enterprise on the Burin Peninsula.

Streets in the making, at Arnold's Cove, Placentia Bay, c. 1967-8. A designated growth center, Arnold's Cove was an outport transformed by the resettlement program of the 1960s.

One of two provincial government resettlement barges, arriving in Arnold's Cove with a house from Harbour Buffett, Long Island, Placentia Bay, 1974.

The last ore was mined at St. Lawrence in 1977, and the operation shut down in February, 1978.

"Lorne home from Ontario," by Newfoundland artist Sidney Butt, 1978.

Transportation

THE OPENING UP of Newfoundland, so long desired by her people, became an accomplished fact after 1949. A road-building program was undertaken, its centrepiece being the Trans-Canada highway, a great boon to the province's contractors and a major artery of commerce. Its paving was completed in 1965, amidst great fanfare. Signs read: "We'll finish the drive in '65."

There were also accomplishments in the air. Starting as a bush operation, Eastern Provincial Airways became the indispensable link between the island and Labrador, spreading its wings in due course westward to Toronto. The helicopter, an essential tool of modern frontier exploration and development, also became a familiar sight in the province's skies.

Older services were adapted to these changes. Passenger service by rail across the island was ended in 1969 and a bus service begun. Coastal boat services were similarly revised as more and more communities were drawn into the expanding road network. By contrast, the ferry service between Port aux Basques and North Sydney was greatly expanded, and a new seasonal connection was introduced between the Nova Scotia port and Argentia.

In the interior of Labrador, short roads were built to serve the needs of specific resource ventures, and a few coastal connections were made. A trans-Labrador highway - the "freedom road" - was planned, but thirty years after Confederation it remained a dream.

Queen's Cove-Northern Bight crossing on the Cabot Highway, Trinity Bay, 1949.

PAC/PA128020/NFB

Paving crew at work. Asphalt was not just something to drive on in post-Confederation Newfoundland, but a way to political success.

DREE

TERRA TRANSPORT

A late shot of the trans-island passenger train, called affectionately "The Bullet." The passenger service was ended by Canadian National in July, 1969.

Busses for the new trans-island passenger service of Canadian National, on the production line of the Prevost Car Co., Ste-Claire, Quebec.

TERRA TRANSPORT

Eastern Provincial Airways was started in 1949 by Eric Blackwood, a Newfoundland-born RCAF veteran, and Chesley Crosbie. From a bush operation, using small aircraft such as the one shown here, it expanded rapidly, absorbing Maritime Central Airways in 1963. With its main base of operations at Gander, EPA is today the regional air carrier of Atlantic Canada.

EASTERN PROVINCIAL AIRWAYS

Welfare State

NEWFOUNDLAND BECAME A PROVINCE of Canada in the era of the social welfare state. Old age pensions had been instituted in Canada in 1927, unemployment insurance in 1940, and family allowances in 1944. In 1949 Newfoundland received the benefit of all these, together with greatly augmented allowances for war veterans. In 1956 legislation was passed by the Parliament of Canada to extend unemployment insurance to fishermen. The same year, a children's health and hospital plan was introduced by the provincial government; and in 1958, with federal support, hospitalization coverage was extended to the entire population.

In such matters Newfoundland was a Canadian leader, not a laggard. The crowning achievement in this policy direction in Newfoundland, as elsewhere in Canada, was the introduction of medicare in 1969. In the 1970s questions of environmental health protection and worker safety took on a new urgency in the province, though the pride of achievement that had characterized the beginnings of the welfare state was perhaps, under the corrosive impact of inflation, giving way there, as elsewhere, to more of a cost-benefit approach.

PAC/PA128803/NFB

Filing clerks at work, Family Allowance office, St. John's, January, 1949.

PAC/PA128016/NFB

Eye examination, Newfoundland school, 1949.

Dr. William Collingwood of the Newfoundland Health Department ship *Lady Anderson*, visiting Red Island, Placentia Bay, 1954.

PAC/PA128067/NFB

First appointees to the
Newfoundland Medical Care
Commission, April 1, 1969. They
are, left to right: Dr. H.M.
Thomey; Dr. J.A. McNamara;
Peter J. Gardiner, chairman;
Roy L. Cheeseman; and James J.
Halley.

Plaque in the lobby of the
Workers' Compensation
Building, St. John's.

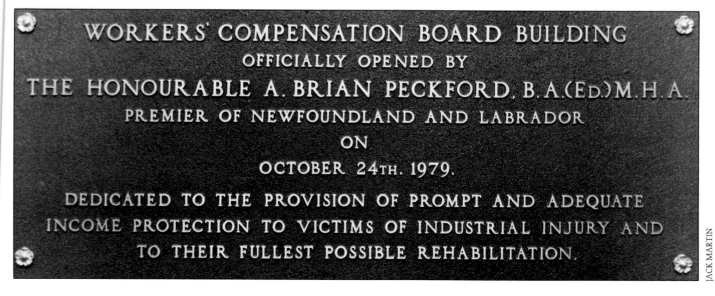

WORKERS' COMPENSATION BOARD BUILDING
OFFICIALLY OPENED BY
THE HONOURABLE A. BRIAN PECKFORD, B.A.(ED.)M.H.A.
PREMIER OF NEWFOUNDLAND AND LABRADOR
ON
OCTOBER 24TH. 1979.
DEDICATED TO THE PROVISION OF PROMPT AND ADEQUATE
INCOME PROTECTION TO VICTIMS OF INDUSTRIAL INJURY AND
TO THEIR FULLEST POSSIBLE REHABILITATION.

Local Government

THE COMMISSION OF GOVERNMENT had encouraged local autonomy, and Windsor had become Newfoundland's second organized municipality in 1938, St. John's having achieved city status in 1921. After Confederation this trend continued. By the early 1980s there were more than three hundred municipal organizations in the province. These included two cities – Corner Brook had been thus elevated in 1955 – and many towns and communities. A metropolitan government was created for the region adjoining St. John's in 1963, and regional government for the entire north-eastern Avalon was contemplated in the 1970s.

Local development associations, lobbies for regional advancement, and a Federation of Municipalities also came to prominence through this process of change. A further wrinkle to local government in Newfoundland was the passing by the legislature of a School Tax Act in 1954, enabling any local area to introduce this form of taxation. A School Tax Authority was established in Corner Brook in 1955, and by the 1980s such authorities were functioning in many parts of the province.

Dorothy Wyatt, R.N., mayor of St. John's, 1974-81.

Town Hall, Jersey Side, Placentia.

Labour

IN 1937 THE GROWTH OF UNIONS in Newfoundland led to the founding of the first enduring Newfoundland Federation of Labour (NFL). (J.R. Smallwood had formed a short-lived organization bearing that name in 1925.) During the war, the commission of government restricted strikes and lockouts, but full employment and prosperity produced a relatively tranquil labour scene. After Confederation favourable legislation encouraged the growth of organized labour, but a tense and revealing confrontation in 1959 between Smallwood on one side and the International Woodworkers of America and the NFL on the other, highlighted underlying difficulties. It was this episode which led to the formation in 1959 of the Newfoundland Democratic Party, which the Federation backed.

In the 1960s and '70s public sector unions and associations grew rapidly in Newfoundland as they did elsewhere in Canada, and labour relations generally in the province entered a new phase of importance. Professional bodies also grew apace, one of the most successful being the Newfoundland Teachers' Association, a nursery for provincial politics. In 1970 workers in the oldest of Newfoundland's industries asserted themselves anew through the formation of the Newfoundland Fishermen, Food and Allied Workers Union (NFFAWU). In labour matters, as in so much else, Newfoundland was becoming a province *comme les autres*.

Annual General Meeting, Newfoundland Teachers' Association, Gander, 1981. The speaker is Paschal Chisholm, president, Canadian Teachers' Federation.

Voting at the third biennial convention of the Newfoundland Association of Public Employees, 1979.

Founding convention of the NFFAWU, April, 1971. Included are, left to right, Fred Dowling, National Director of the Canadian Food and Allied Workers' Union; Fr. Desmond McGrath; Alec Brown; Richard Cashin, President of the NFFAWU; and Woodrow Philpott. The new union was an amalgamation of the provincial arm of the Canadian Food and Allied Workers' Union and the locally formed Northern Fishermen's Union.

Education

THE DENOMINATIONAL CHARACTER of schooling inherited in Newfoundland from the nineteenth century was confirmed by the Terms of Union with Canada in 1948. But rapid expansion thereafter brought new influences to bear upon the system. Like all large educational systems, Newfoundland's moved in secular and bureaucratic directions, though its outward appearance made it seem unique. A prominent feature of education after 1949 was the consolidation of schools, which necessitated an elaborate bus network.

A fresh start was also made at the post-secondary level. Memorial University College became a degree-granting institution in 1949 and began an expansion that gave it national status. It moved to a new campus in 1961. Some of its old buildings were eventually occupied by the College of Fisheries, Navigation, Marine Engineering, and Technology. Founded in 1964, this imaginative institution offered a curriculum well suited to regional needs. A network of vocational schools was also created in the province, the largest being the College of Trades and Technology in St. John's. In 1975 Memorial University opened a regional college, subsequently named in honour of Sir Wilfred Grenfell, at Corner Book; and in 1977 Bay St. George Community College was opened in Stephenville.

Classroom, Pouch Cove, 1948.

Typical school scene, 1981.

Students from the College of Fisheries, Navigation, Marine Engineering and Technology at lifeboat training.

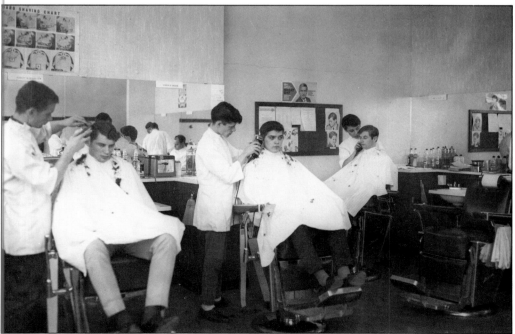

Learning to barber, College of Trades and Technology, St. John's.

Communications

RADIO WAS WELL ESTABLISHED in Newfoundland by the time of Confederation and Newfoundlanders had shown themselves to be great talkers and listeners, bringing to the airwaves their rich traditions of speech and lore. The first public telecast in Newfoundland was made in 1955, and the province's first television personality was Don Jamieson. The building of the trans-Canada microwave network brought live television and a greatly improved long-distance telephone service to the island. The electronic media provided yet another avenue into politics.

Interestingly, while the province was hooked up to outside networks from an early date, it was not overwhelmed by them and it was not until 1977 that cable service was introduced, stepping up the flow of American programming. Gander maintained its status as a major centre of world communication through its air traffic control functions, which encompassed much of the north-western Atlantic region.

The newspaper scene in the province was dominated after 1949, as before, by the two St. John's dailies, the *Daily News* and *Evening Telegram*, but many community and regional newspapers were established and flourished.

Central switchboard, Canadian
National Telegraph office,
Clarenville, 1949.

Erection of microwave tower,
part of the trans-Canada
network, Corner Brook, 1958.

Bob Cole (right) and Gary Dornhoefer in the gondola, Maple Leaf Gardens, Toronto, 1980. Cole, born in St. John's in 1934, brought a voice from Newfoundland radio to a national TV audience.

Simone Michel, Naskapi-Montagnais resident of Sheshatshit, Labrador, at public hearings in December, 1979, into the environmental and social impact of a proposed uranium mine to be operated by Brinex. "Is it the purpose of the mine to destroy our culture?" he is asking.

Don Jamieson, broadcaster extraordinaire. Born in St. John's in 1921, best known on local television for his CJON program "News Cavalcade," he made an easy step into federal politics in 1966, and was successively Minister of Defence Production, Minister of Transport, Minister of Regional Economic Expansion, Minister of Industry, Trade and Commerce, and Secretary of State for External Affairs in the government of Canada.

The Life of the Mind

Post-Confederation Newfoundland, especially in the 1970s, witnessed an unprecedented flowering of artistic, literary, and scientific endeavour. The region had long attracted artists to its stunning seascapes; it now produced a sizeable artistic community of its own, whose talent found expression in many genres. Writing, which had deep native roots in Newfoundland, also had a burst of creativity and was nurtured by an expanded readership and enterprising local publishers. In scholarship, Memorial University developed an exciting regional focus in the arts, social sciences, and other disciplines.

There was also a rediscovery of traditional Newfoundland culture in all its manifestations. On stage the province's ways were tellingly transmitted to the larger world by old performers and new. Newfoundland, in short, became a widely understood backdrop for the literary and artistic imagination. Regionally flavoured figures had great success in both Canada and the United States. The federal and provincial governments encouraged these developments, and in 1980 the work of the national granting agencies was complemented by the creation of the Newfoundland and Labrador Arts Council. Governments, too, spent massively on the building up of a public scientific establishment in Newfoundland to service the region's economy.

BRIAN WILLER/MACLEAN'S

Working in greatly contrasting styles, Newfoundland artists Mary and Christopher Pratt have won international recognition.

Harold Horwood. Born in St. John's in 1923, his diverse career has touched many aspects of the life of the province. His novel *Tomorrow Will Be Sunday* (1966) is the most ambitious fictional representation of outport life to be attempted since 1949. In *The Foxes of Beachy Cove* (1967) his talent as a naturalist was revealed in a minor classic of observation and meditation.

ETV/MUN

DICTIONARY OF NFLD. ENGLISH/MUN

Professors G.M. Story and William Kirwin, working at Memorial University on the *Dictionary of Newfoundland English*, a unique enterprise in the humanities, which they edited with J.D.A Widdowson. In 1979 Story was named to be the first chairman of the Newfoundland and Labrador Arts Council.

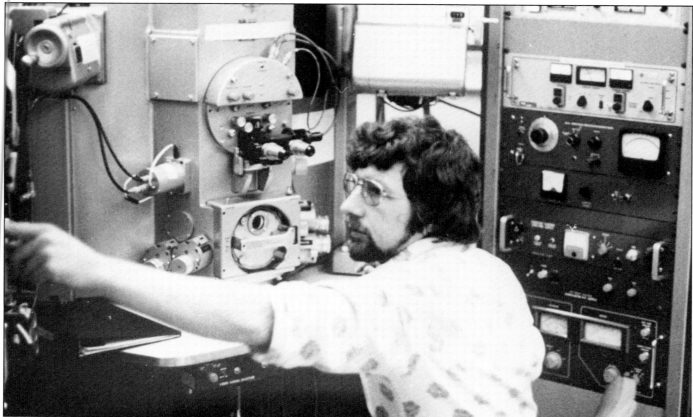

Newfoundlander Rex Gibbons, operating an electron microprobe machine analyzing samples of moon rocks at NASA's Lyndon B. Johnson Space Center, Houston, Texas, 1975.

Grand Falls native Gordon Pinsent, actor, author, and director, one of Canada's most versatile performers on stage and screen.

Greg Malone as "Mr. Budgell." Born in St. John's in 1948, Malone has been working in theatre since 1971. "Mr. Budgell" is the fictional manager of the Wonderful Grand Band, a musical and theatrical group formed in 1978.

194

Rufus Guinchard (left) and Emile Benoit, Newfoundland fiddlers. Guinchard was born at Daniel's Harbour, Great Northern Peninsula, and Benoit at Black Duck Brook on the Port au Port Peninsula.

John Joe English of Job's Cove, Conception Bay, storyteller, singer, and reciter.

Outdoors

A PARKS MOVEMENT in post-Confederation Newfoundland laid the basis for much enjoyment of the province's natural beauties. The first provincial parks act was passed in 1952, and the first park in what became a large system was established in 1954 near Corner Brook; it was named in honour of Sir Richard Squires. Terra Nova National Park was established on the east coast of the island in 1957, and the Gros Morne National Park, which encompasses part of the Long Range Mountains, was established on the west coast in 1970.

The federal government also developed a number of historical parks and promoted restoration and explanatory historical marking. By the 1970s the province's development of historical sites was also notable, as was the revival of the Newfoundland Museum in St. John's and the work of various local museums. Labrador benefited less from all this, but in the early 1980s a national park was projected for the region.

An outing in Sir Richard Squires Memorial Park soon after its opening.

Part of the Main

By THE 1970s and '80s much was known about Newfoundland and Labrador; yet much remained to be discovered. In 1978 a climbing party reached a peak in the Torngat Mountains of northern Labrador, whose height turned out to be greater than any previously recorded in the province. The following year oil flowed from beneath the ocean floor at the Hibernia P-15 discovery well, approximately 265 kilometres southeast of St. John's on the Grand Banks. Newfoundland was once more poised for great change, her people looking beyond the headlands to the ocean that had first nurtured their society. But the *Ocean Ranger* disaster of February, 1982, was a reminder that even in the age of high technology the sea remained "an edge for human grief."

Ray Chipeniuk and Ron Parker on the summit of "L1" (i.e. Labrador 1) in the Torngat mountains, 1978.

Sweet Newfoundland crude.

197

Hibernia Well P-15.

The *Ocean Ranger*, in its day one of the largest semi-submersible oil rigs in the world, sank on the Grand Banks on February 15, 1982, with a loss of eighty-four lives. "Full many a year shall pass ere they're forgot."

On April 12, 1980, Terry Fox of Port Coquitlam, British Columbia, who had lost a leg to cancer, set out from St. John's to run across Canada. His effort stirred the country. He is shown here in front of City Hall, St. John's, wearing the mayor's robe and chain.

DICK GREEN

"Their treasure is, and ever
shall be, stored in its generous
depths. Where their treasure is,
there is their heart also."
(Richard Howley, 1887.)

FURTHER READING

CELL, GILLIAN T., *English Enterprise in Newfoundland 1577-1660* (Toronto, University of Toronto Press, 1969)

CELL, GILLIAN T., ed., *Newfoundland Discovered: English Attempts at Colonisation, 1610-1630* (London, The Hakluyt Society, 1982)

GUNN, GERTRUDE E., *The Political History of Newfoundland 1832-1864* (Toronto, University of Toronto Press, 1966)

HALPERT, HERBERT, AND STORY, G.M., eds., *Christmas Mumming in Newfoundland* (Toronto, University of Toronto Press, 1970)

HEAD, C. GRANT, *Eighteenth Century Newfoundland: A Geographer's Perspective* (Toronto, McClelland and Stewart, 1976)

HILLER, JAMES, AND NEARY, PETER, eds., *Newfoundland in the Nineteenth and Twentieth Centuries: Essays in Interpretation* (Toronto, University of Toronto Press, 1980)

MANNION, JOHN, ed., *The Peopling of Newfoundland: Essays in Historical Geography* (St. John's, Memorial University, 1977)

MATTHEWS, KEITH, *Lectures on the History of Newfoundland: 1500-1830* (St. John's, Memorial University, 1973)

NOEL, S.J.R., *Politics in Newfoundland* (Toronto, University of Toronto Press, 1971)

O'FLAHERTY, PATRICK, *The Rock Observed: Studies in the Literature of Newfoundland* (Toronto, University of Toronto Press, 1979)

O'NEILL, PAUL, *The Story of St. John's, Newfoundland*; Vol. I, *The Oldest City*; Vol. II, *A Seaport Legacy* (Erin, Ontario, Press Porcepic, 1975, 1976)

ROSE, CLYDE, ed., *The Blasty Bough* (St. John's, Breakwater Books, 1976)

ROWE, F.W., *A History of Newfoundland and Labrador* (Toronto, McGraw-Hill Ryerson, 1980)

SMALLWOOD, JOSEPH R., ed., *Encyclopedia of Newfoundland and Labrador*, Vol. I (St. John's, Nfld. Book Publishers, 1981)

STORY, G.M., KIRWIN, W.J., AND WIDDOWSON, J.D.A., *Dictionary of Newfoundland English* (Toronto, University of Toronto Press, 1982)

TUCK, JAMES, *Newfoundland and Labrador Prehistory* (Ottawa, National Museum of Man, 1976)

ABBREVIATIONS

CNS   Centre for Newfoundland Studies, Queen Elizabeth II Library, Memorial University

ETV   Educational Television, Photography Division, Memorial University

MUN   Memorial University of Newfoundland

NFB   National Film Board of Canada

NQ   *Newfoundland Quarterly*

PAC   Public Archives of Canada

PANL   Provincial Archives of Newfoundland and Labrador

PRO   Public Record Office, London

ACKNOWLEDGEMENTS

The authors have made every effort to identify, credit appropriately, and obtain publication rights from copyright holders of illustrations in this book. Notice of any errors or omissions in this regard will be gratefully received, and corrections made in any subsequent edition.

The following pictures are here acknowledged in the form of words required by their owners: for the PRO illustrations, Crown copyright material in the Public Record Office is reproduced by permission of the Controller of Her Majesty's Stationery Office; James Blaine, Henry Cabot Lodge, and John Hay, copyright National Portrait Gallery, Smithsonian Institution, Washington, D.C.; R.T.S. Lowell, from THE LOWELLS AND THEIR SEVEN WORLDS by Ferris Greenslet. Copyright 1946 by Ferris Greenslet. Copyright © renewed 1973 by Magdalena Greenslet Finley. Reprinted by permission of Houghton Mifflin Company; the illustration from Cassini's *Voyage* is Courtesy of the Edward E. Ayer Collection, The Newberry Library, Chicago; the Beothuck canoe from the journal of the *Indeavour*, copyright His Grace the Archbishop of Canterbury and the Trustees of Lambeth Palace Library; two Duncan Macpherson cartoons and photo including J.W. Pickersgill are Reprinted with permission – the Toronto Star; the photo of Cary and Cole, Courtesy William A. Farnsworth Library and Art Museum, Rockland, Maine; Lord Baltimore's letter, copyright Arents Collections, The New York Public Library, Astor, Lenox and Tilden Foundations; the Dunbar poem is extracted By permission of the Master and Fellows, Magdalene College, Cambridge; Thomas Cochrane, copyright National Maritime Museum by kind permission Hon. Mrs. G. Hastings; two oil paintings of Trinity, and paintings of George and Amy Garland, courtesy the Dorset Natural History & Archaeological Society, Dorset County Museum, Dorchester, England; the great auk, Courtesy of the Royal Ontario Museum, Toronto, Canada; the W. Hind drawing, courtesy J. Ross Robertson Collection, Metropolitan Toronto Library; and the montage "The Living Fathers of Confederation" is reprinted by permission of Macmillan of Canada A Division of Gage Publishing Limited. Other credit lines accompany the illustrations throughout the book. Quotations from the work of E.J. Pratt are by permission of Claire Pratt (prose) and the University of Toronto Press (poetry).

In addition, we would like to thank the following for their help: H.J. McGonigal and E.J. Coady, DREE; Robert Bockstael, M.P.; W.A.B. Douglas, Directorate of History, National Defence H.Q.; Richard Bond, Fisheries & Oceans Canada; Kay Philpott, Canadian Wildlife Service; Hon. James Morgan, Minister of Fisheries, Nfld.; Hon. Wallace House, Minister of Health, Nfld.; Eric Rowe and Desmond Sullivan, Premier's Office, Nfld.; Dr. Rex Gibbons, Nfld. Dept. of Mines & Energy; Donald Johnson and Don Hustins, Nfld. Dept. of Culture, Recreation & Youth; Wayne Sturge, Nfld. Dept. of Development; Kenneth Harnum, Nfld. Dept. of Rural, Agricultural & Northern Development; Cec Roebothan, Nfld. Dept. of Education; H. Dondenaz, Historical Services, Air Canada; Gary Callahan, Terra Transport; Susan Sherk, Mobil; C.F. Armstrong, CN Holdings; K.J. MacDonald, Canadian National Communications; H.R. Steele, EPA; Charles Bursey, Nfld. & Labrador Hydro; Bill Moyse, Canadian Saltfish Corp.; Wayne Noseworthy, NTA; Nancy Riche, NAPE; Diane Hogan, Tom Ronayne, and Drs. Ben Hogan and Alex Balisch, Nfld. Transportation Historical Society; Malcolm McLaren, CBC; Robert McGhee, National Museums of Canada; William Fitzhugh, Smithsonian Institution; Harry Cuff, N*fld. Quarterly*; H.P. Wood, *Atlantic Advocate*; Rev. Timothy Watson, Intercontinental Church Society; I. Baldauf, Archiv der Brüder-Unität, Herrnhut; Maj. Herbert I. Fraser and Christine Ardern, Salvation Army; Dean E.C.W. Rusted; Archbishop Alphonsus Penney; Sister Teresa Francis, Presentation Convent; Sister Mary Edwardine, Mercy Convent; Rev. Burton K. Janes, Pentecostal Assemblies of Nfld.; Edythe Goodridge, G.M. Story, William Kirwin, G.O. Roberts, Lieda Bell, Shane O'Dea, Melvin Baker, Robert Rogerson, Shannon Ryan, Barbara Starcher, Edward-Vincent

Chafe, John Mannion, Roger Clark, James Tuck, Edith Bosak, William Montevecchi, and Ernst Deutsch of Memorial University; Erich Hahn, Fred Armstrong, Roger Hall, Samuel Clark, Paul Potter, K.H.W. Hilborn, Jeanette Berry, Rosie Brazier, Chris Speed, and Carmen Callon of the University of Western Ontario; Dick Green, Chief Justice Robert Furlong, Hon. J.W. Pickersgill, Hon. J.R. Smallwood, Alan Wilson, David Higgs, R.D.W. Pitt, C.M. Lane, D. Peter Hegler, Gertrude Crosbie, Doris Saunders, Beate Gundert, Burnham Gill, Eric Beyreuther, Capt. D.C. Fraser, Anne Reed, David Reed, A.P. Bates, Jock Bates, John Moyse, Robert Cole, Keith O'Neill, Frank Galgay, Paul O'Neill, Frank Graham, Mrs. M. R. Lee, and Rev. F.W. Peacock. Though long, this list is not exhaustive, and we would like to thank all others who assisted us in our enterprise.

Index